ELEPHANT
MOUNTAIN

ART BOUDREAU

Cover Art by
Richard Charles

Olympus Story House
www.olympusstoryhouse.com

Table of Contents

For My Wife ~ Bernardine

My Dad ~ Bruno and In Remembrance of My Mom ~ Ruth

My Sister ~ Betty and Her Angel ~ Ruthann

My Daughters ~ Calla ~ Garnett ~ Amber

And Our Special Angel ~ Trinity Elizabeth

My Close Friends ~ Ross and Tony

For Their Belief In Me, Encouragement And Support

And For All The People Who Have Problems Reading

My thanks to Trafford Publishing, the BC Ministry of Advanced Education's 'Learners Talking to Learners Event' grant, the Victoria READ Society, my teacher, Helen, my tutors, especially Danda and Elinor, and my classmates, John, Glenn, Kendal, Peter, Liz and Sarah for all their help and support in making it possible for this book to be published. *{And specal thanks to those classmates who gave up a whale watching adventure to give their wholehearted support and energy to share this adventure with me.}*

I want to especially thank my wife for all her hours and hours of support and patience throughout my hours of writing and editing. It has been a long and interesting journey.

No doubt the Universe is unfolding as it should...

The Victoria READ Society (READ) is a non-profit literacy organization; founded in 1976 to help students of all ages in the Greater Victoria area learn basic academic skills through small classes, individualized help and a supportive, caring environment. READ currently provides full-time adult literacy classes, ESL and literacy services for newcomers to Canada, and programs for children on a one-on-one basis.

Chapter One

An old prospector told me about a young Irishman named Paddy Peacock who came to Canada from Ireland in the early 1890s to get rich. He came to the little town of Nelson by train from Vancouver to look for gold in the mountains of BC.

The train ride was dry and dusty. As Paddy walked up the street, he could see a saloon. He could use a good drink of whiskey. When he reached the saloon, he stopped to bang some of the dust from his clothes.

"Young man, is that gold dust that you're banging off your clothes?"

Paddy looked up and saw a big man standing in the doorway of the saloon. "No, it's the dust that came with the train ride."

"What's your name, young man?"

"Paddy Peacock, I just got in town."

"Paddy Peacock. Well, we have to give you a new name, young man. Will you stop banging the dust off your clothes? It looks like gold dust in the sun. That's it! Gold Dust will be your new name. They call me O'Donald. I'm the blacksmith in town."

"Gold Dust, I like that name, O'Donald."

"Come in and have a drink, Gold Dust, I'm buying."

"I can use a drink, O'Donald."

The two men walked into the saloon and over to a table in the corner. It was loud and smoky, and smelled of liquor. There were prospectors at the card tables, some dancing girls, and some working girls.

"Well, Gold Dust, what do you think of this?"

"Is it like this all the time?"

"That it is, young man. What is a little Irishman like you doing in these mountains?"

"I came to get rich."

O'Donald laughed at Paddy, "It's all gone."

"There must be a little gold in them mountains for me?"

"The only way you'll find gold is if you're lucky."

"I have the luck of forty Irishmen."

The two men had a good laugh. Gold Dust had two drinks with O'Donald and then said, "I have to go and get some supplies."

"Okay, Gold Dust, when you're done, come over to my shop."

"Okay, I'll do that."

When Gold Dust walked out of the saloon, he stopped and looked up at the nearest mountain.

As he walked down the street, he was thinking,

"Gold Dust, that sounds like a lucky name." He could see the blacksmith's shop, the hotel and the store as he walked along. Then he could see the stables. He would need a mule to carry his packs.

When he reached the stables, an old man came out.

"Can I help you, young man?"

"Hi, my name's Gold Dust."

"They call me Snowcap. You're new in town. Who gave you the name Gold Dust?"

"O'Donald did."

"That's something he would do. What can I do for you?"

"I need a good mule."

"I have one mule and no one will buy him, because he has a mind of his own."

"How much for that lazy mule? He's not moving around much."

"You give me ten dollars, and you can have him. I don't have the money to feed him all winter."

"Sold! Here's ten dollars."

"There he is, see if you can get him to move."

"What's his name?"

"I call him Dumb Mule."

"I guess I need a new name for him."

"Good luck with that dumb mule, you're going to need it."

Chapter Two

As Gold Dust walked with his mule over to the store, he was thinking of a lucky name for his mule. Then it dawned on him, "I'll call him Paddy. That's a lucky name for a mule. Mule, your name will be Paddy."

He tied Paddy to a rail outside the store and went in to get his supplies. As he walked over to the blacksmith shop, he could see O'Donald standing at the front of it.

"There is no gold for you; it is all gone!"

Gold Dust smiled at the big Irishman. "I told you I have the luck of forty Irishmen," Gold Dust chuckled, "and I have my lucky mule, Paddy."

The two men had a laugh. Gold Dust sat down and asked O'Donald, "What's the name of that mountain?"

"That's Elephant Mountain."

"That's a good name for that mountain, O'Donald."

"Did you get all your supplies, young man?"

"I have to wait for a pick and shovel to come in by train in four days."

"Well, young man, you're going to need a gun to keep the wild animals away, and the men that like to rob poor prospectors because they're too damn lazy to dig their own gold."

"I don't have enough money to buy a gun. You think I need one, O'Donald?"

"Yup, there's always someone getting robbed for their gold."

"Well, I'll have to get some gold before I can buy a gun, and just hope I don't get robbed before then."

"Young man, you know we Irish must keep together. There's not many of us in Nelson."

"I haven't seen any in this town."

"Just me and you, Gold Dust. Come in the shop, I'll tell you of some spots that have been worked hard."

"Okay, O'Donald."

"Maybe you could find a little gold in those spots. I've got an old map around here that I used when I came here to look for gold. You can have it."

"Thanks, O'Donald."

"Here it is. I marked some spots where I looked for gold."

"Did you make any money, O'Donald?"

"Enough in one year to buy this shop, but not enough to get me back home to Ireland."

"You want to go back home to Ireland?"

"I don't want to die here in this hell-hole, Gold Dust."

"I'm a little homesick and I've only been in Canada for one month."

"Enough of being homesick, let's get you ready. I've got an old pick and a shovel in the back of my shop."

"How much you want for them?"

"You can have them. I don't need them anymore."

"Thank you, O'Donald."

"Gold Dust, come and sit down."

"Okay."

"Let's have a drink of good Irish whiskey. It looks like you need one, Gold Dust."

"Yup, I think I do, O'Donald, maybe even two."

The two men sat and drank half a bottle of whiskey. They talked about Ireland and Nelson and how gold made some men kill for it.

"Well, Gold Dust, we need to find you a gun."

"I have no money to buy a gun, O'Donald."

"Young man, you're not listening to me. I said we have to *find* you a gun, not *buy* you a gun."

"Who's going to give me a gun?"

"You're still not listening to what I said. Find a gun. I have two in here under this hay. We have to dig in the hay and find them."

"Now I know what you meant, find a gun."

The two men dug in the hay looking for the two guns. "O'Donald, I've found a bottle of whiskey. You must have lost it in the hay."

"That's where I lost that damn bottle two years ago! Let's stop and have a drink, Gold Dust."

"That's a good idea, O'Donald. Maybe it will help us find the guns, and it won't hurt."

The two men had three more drinks, and went back looking for the guns. "Gold Dust, you think you're going to find the mother lode?"

"I'm going to find it, O'Donald, I'm going to."

"When you do, you think you could lend me enough to go home?"

"That I can do, O'Donald, and you'll go back in style."

"Thanks. You're a good man, Gold Dust. Here's that old rifle. It has to be cleaned, but it's a good gun. That Colt 45 should be around here."

"Here's the Colt 45. It's a nice gun, O'Donald, and here are two boxes of bullets."

"Let's clean them, and I'll teach you how to use your guns."

"You said my guns."

"You were listening this time. Yes, you can have them. I don't use them any more, but I was a very good shot when I did."

"I can't take your guns!"

"Yes, you can."

"I have to pay you for them, O'Donald."

"All you have to do is remember me when you get rich."

"I'll remember you and I will get you home in style. I will, O'Donald."

"Let's clean the guns."

After cleaning the guns they went to the back of O'Donald's shop and put up a target. They shot at the target until dark, then went back to O'Donald's shop and lit two lanterns.

"You're a good shot, Gold Dust, for a young man."

"My dad took me hunting. He told me to shoot at the chest, it would stop any animal."

"You can have a place to sleep in the shop for as long as you want."

"Thanks, O'Donald, for all your kindness. You're like a dad to me."

"That's enough; you're going to make me cry. Go and find a spot to put your bed."

"Thanks again, you're making my life a little easier than it would be."

"Well, you remind me of my son. He was killed by a robber. It happened when I came to town to get some dynamite. When I got back he was dead, shot in the head. That damn robber tied his hands and shot him. He was your age, just a kid."

"I didn't know."

"That's okay, one day I'll find that damn robber and kill him like he killed my son. He stole a pocket watch that my dad gave my son. And I walked by him on my way back to my camp! I remember that damn robber's face, just like it was yesterday."

"You'll find him, O'Donald, and I'll help you kill him."

"Let's have something to eat, Gold Dust. It's been a long day."

"Okay, that sounds good."

Then they sat and had something to eat. After they ate, O'Donald pulled out a bottle of Irish whiskey. The two men sat and talked. O'Donald had been in Nelson for six years. He and his son looked for gold for about a year. Then his son was murdered.

The next morning, Gold Dust was all fired-up to dig for gold. He had his mule packed but had to wait for O'Donald to wake up. When O'Donald woke up and walked out of his shop he stopped, looked at Gold Dust and began laughing, "Gold Dust, slow down. Go and get some bullets for the guns and come back to the shop."

When Gold Dust got back to the shop he couldn't see O'Donald. "Where are you, O'Donald?"

"Behind the shop, come back and help me."

"Okay, I got some bullets. What do you need a hand with?"

"Give me a hand with this old sluice. I used it when I was looking for gold."

"I can't believe my eyes. It's small enough to go on the mule."

"Take the sluice and when you hit it big, send me back to Ireland."

"You're like a lucky horseshoe!"

"I have some old dynamite in here somewhere. There it is. Help me dig it out. Gold Dust, do not blow yourself up."

"I won't, O'Donald."

"All you have to do is put a stick in a hole, light the fuse and run."

"That's not too hard to do."

As the two men said good-bye, Gold Dust told O'Donald that he would pay him for all his kindness. O'Donald told him again, "When you get rich, then you can pay me back by paying for me to go back to Ireland."

Gold Dust smiled, "You have a deal, and I will see you in one month."

Chapter Three

As Gold Dust walked out of the town with Paddy, he looked up at Elephant Mountain. He could see the shape of an elephant and it seemed to look back at him. He smiled and kept walking along the west arm of the lake to Five Mile Creek.

Then he turned and walked up a deer trail into the forest where he found a small stream. He made camp and put up the sluice. Then he began digging sand from the stream into the sluice. It was hard work. By the end of the day he had four small nuggets and very little gold dust. His back and hands hurt like hell. He was happy he had some gold for his first day.

The next morning Gold Dust had some coffee and something to eat. Then he went back to work looking for more gold in that little stream. By lunch, he had four good-sized gold nuggets and some gold dust. By dark, he had ten more nuggets and some more gold dust. He was a happy man to have found some gold his first two days as a gold prospector.

He sat and ate some beans and pork. He was thinking that he would have to go into town and stake a claim. If he left his camp, someone might work his claim or steal his sluice when he was gone. He would stay and work the claim for the month.

Every night after dark Gold Dust would hide his gold in a hole under a big fir tree about one hundred yards from his camp. By week three he had worked up and down the stream looking for gold, moving the sluice and camp ten times. There was very little gold left in the stream. He would stay and work the stream hard for one more week. He used his gold pan and worked up and down the little stream. He found very little gold in his last week, just a little gold dust.

His last night at his camp, just before going to bed, he could hear someone coming up the deer trail. It was two men with two mules. Gold Dust grabbed his gun. He didn't want to be robbed. "That's far enough. What do you men want?"

"Can we make some coffee on your fire? We're going up to the lake at the top of the mountain to look for gold."

"Come on up, make yourselves at home."

"Thanks. They call me One Eye Jack, and that's Ace getting the coffee."

"I'm Gold Dust. You can use my coffee pot. The water in the stream makes good coffee."

"Thanks, Gold Dust, we have a long walk up to the lake."

The two men stayed for a good hour talking and smoking. As the fire died down, they picked up their cups and coffee. "We have to go now, Gold Dust."

Then they walked away into the dark under the big trees in the forest. Gold Dust could see the light of the lantern moving up the hill and then it was gone. Then Gold Dust went to bed with his gun like every night for the past month. And like every night for the past month, he dreamed of Elephant Mountain.

In the morning, he packed up camp and his sluice and started back to town. On his walk back, he was thinking of a hot bath and a good woman. He kept looking up at Elephant Mountain and thinking, "Could there be gold on that mountain?"

Chapter Four

When Gold Dust reached the town, he walked over to O'Donald's shop. O'Donald could see Gold Dust coming towards him. O'Donald smiled and laughed, and Gold Dust laughed back at him. The two men shook hands. "Gold Dust, you look like shit."

"I feel like shit."

"You could use a bath and clean clothes. Let's have a drink or two."

"Okay, that sounds good."

The two men sat talking for about an hour.

"Gold Dust, go and sell your gold. I'll put a fire under the tub. It should be hot when you get back."

"Thanks, O'Donald, you don't have to do that."

"I know, but I want to, Gold Dust, it will make me happy."

"Okay, if it makes you happy. I'll go and sell my gold."

"I'll take care of Paddy and have a look at his shoes."

Gold Dust went and sold his gold. He had more gold than he thought he had, much more. He was a very happy man. When Gold Dust got back to the shop, the water in the tub was hot. "Thanks, O'Donald."

"Did you hit the mother lode?"

"No, but enough to get a good woman and have some fun tonight."

"That's good, but you should hide some of your money. Those women at the saloon and card tables will take all your money in one night."

"You sound like my dad, O'Donald."

"I'm just looking out for you, Gold Dust."

"I'll hide some and put some in the bank."

"That's a good man. Now have your bath, I'm going over to the saloon to bullshit and have a drink."

Gold Dust had his bath, a shave and put clean clothes on. He hid some of his money and put some in the bank. Then he walked over to the saloon. When he got in the saloon, he looked for O'Donald. He was in the corner with two women and called out, "Come over here, Gold Dust, and meet the girls. This redhead is Lucky, and her friend is Happy."

"Morning girls, I'm Gold Dust."

The girls went back to work. Gold Dust and O'Donald sat and talked over some whiskey about where he found his gold and if he should go back to the same place. Then Gold Dust asked O'Donald about Elephant Mountain, "Do you think there's gold on that mountain?"

"No one has found any on Elephant Mountain that I know about."

"I keep dreaming of that mountain, O'Donald."

"Maybe there is and no one can find it."

"Are you going to play some cards with me?"

"No, Gold Dust, I have to go back to the shop and do some work. You have fun; I'll see you in the morning."

"Okay, I'll see you in the morning."

Gold Dust had fun in the saloon playing cards and bullshitting with some of the prospectors. The girls were all over Gold Dust because he had money in his pocket. Then next morning Gold Dust woke up with a big head and no money. But when he had gone to sleep he'd had money in his pocket.

As he walked over to the blacksmith shop, he was thinking of what O'Donald told him the day before, that he should hide some of his money because the girls would steal all of it. Thank God he listened to O'Donald the day before or he would have no money at all! O'Donald could see Gold Dust walking up to his shop and stood behind the door with a bucket of cold water. When Gold Dust walked in the shop, O'Donald dumped the water over Gold Dust. "What the hell is going on?"

O'Donald laughed, "That woke you up!"

"I needed a cold bath this morning. Thanks O'Donald."

The two men had a good laugh and talked for a while. Gold Dust told O'Donald about having money when he went to sleep and having no money in the morning.

"Gold Dust, you should go and get your supplies before the crew from the silver mine come to town. They will buy up most of the supplies in town."

"Okay, I'll go and get them now."

"Take the wheelbarrow, Gold Dust, it will make your job easier."

"Thanks again. I'll see you when I get back."

After getting supplies, Gold Dust went back and sat with O'Donald, thanked him again for being like a dad to him, and said that he would pay him back for all his kindness. O'Donald told him again, "When you get rich you can pay my way back to Ireland because I don't want to die here."

"You have a deal, O' Donald."

That afternoon Gold Dust would go to the next valley to look for gold. The two men said goodbye.

"Good luck, Gold Dust, and be careful!"

"I will, O'Donald, I will."

Gold Dust walked with his mule, Paddy, out of Nelson for one month to look for more gold. As he walked up the hill out of town, he stopped and looked at the little town and Elephant Mountain.

It looked like that mountain was looking at him again. Then he kept walking out of town thinking,

"Is there gold on that mountain?"

Chapter Five

As he walked along the trail he met some more prospectors going back to Nelson. One of the prospectors stopped to talk to Gold Dust. "Hi, young man, I'm Pistol Pete!"

"I'm Gold Dust."

"You want to keep your eyes sharp and your pistol handy. There's a robber in the next valley. He shot a prospector dead, took his boots, mule and everything else he could take!"

Gold Dust was not happy to hear about a robber that would kill you for your gold and take your clothes. "Why would a man kill you for gold?"

"Greed, Gold Dust. I have to go now. You watch out!"

"Okay, Pistol Pete. See you around."

As he walked with Paddy, Gold Dust thought about that poor prospector and what he would do if someone tried to rob him. All he could do was to kill the robber. That would be the only way he could stay alive.

Suddenly Paddy stopped and would not move. Gold Dust tried to pull and push Paddy but he would not move. He tried some sugar and two apples but that mule would not move. So Gold Dust sat, had a smoke and looked at that mule and shook his head.

Then he heard a loud noise and the ground started to shake. Gold Dust saw some big rocks tumbling and sliding down the side of the mountain. They covered the trail about one hundred yards in front of him. He looked over at Paddy, "If you hadn't stopped when you did, we would be under that rockslide!" Gold Dust gave Paddy a big kiss and two apples. "Paddy, you're good luck!"

Then Paddy started to walk down the trail to the slide. When they reached the rocks on the trail

Paddy worked his way around and made his own trail through the slide. Gold Dust couldn't believe that Paddy knew that the slide was going to happen and that he could find his way over the slide.

By the time they made camp for the night, the two of them had walked 30 miles. It would be dark in two hours. Gold Dust grabbed his gold pan and walked down to a little creek to pan for gold until dark. He found one small nugget in two hours. Gold Dust put some oats down for Paddy and gave him a small bite of sugar. Then he had something to eat and a good drink of whiskey before going to bed.

Gold Dust lay on his back, looking at the stars. He kept thinking about that poor soul that was shot by a robber, and could he really shoot a man? He knew he had to look out for number one first. Then he fell asleep with his Colt 45.

The next morning, Gold Dust was up before the crows. He made coffee, had a good breakfast and then it was time to go back up to the trail. Gold Dust would have to walk fast to make it to the next valley before dark. As he walked with Paddy along the trail, Gold Dust looked up to the tops of the mountains covered with snow. "Paddy, it could get really cold here in the winter."

They passed prospectors on the trail going back to Nelson. Some prospectors stopped and talked. They all told him that the gold had dried up in the valley. One man told him, "There's still a robber in the valley. You should be careful when working and keep a gun with you at all times."

Then Gold Dust pulled his Colt 45 out of the pack on Paddy and put it on. By the end of the day he was in the valley; they made good time. Paddy stopped. Gold Dust looked at Paddy, "Paddy, we can't camp here, there's three hours of light."

Gold Dust had a smoke.

Paddy started to walk to the north. This wasn't the way that Gold Dust wanted to go, but if Paddy wanted to go north they would go north. They walked for about an hour then came to a small river. Paddy walked down the bank, turned up river and kept walking. Gold Dust couldn't stop Paddy, so he walked with him. It seemed like Paddy knew where he was going.

They came upon an old man digging in the bank of the river for gold. The old prospector had a hole about ten feet into the bank. Paddy stopped, and the old man looked at Gold Dust and Paddy.

The old man began laughing. As he laughed, he walked over to Gold Dust. "I'm not laughing at you; I'm laughing at that mule. I bought that mule six months ago, but that damn mule would go where he wanted to and I couldn't stop him, so I gave him back and got a new mule."

Gold Dust smiled, "Yup, he stops when he wants and goes if he wants to."

"Young man, do you have some coffee and maybe some rum?"

"I have coffee, but no rum."

"My name is Jim Tool. Everyone calls me Old Jim."

"I'm Gold Dust, and that mule is Paddy."

"Go over to my camp and put some wood on the fire. I'll be right there."

When Jim got to his camp, Gold Dust had put some coffee on.

"I ran out of coffee five days ago."

"I have no rum, but I have some whiskey."

"Yes! You're a good young man, Gold Dust. Let's have some of that whiskey, and some coffee. I'm going to town in two days. When I get back, I'll bring you some coffee and rum."

"It's time for me to make camp, Jim."

"My claim ends at the corner, you'll see the stake."

"Thanks, Jim."

"I'll come up before I go to town, Gold Dust."

"Okay, Jim."

Gold Dust walked up the small river around the corner. There was a good spot to make camp for the month to work the river. Gold Dust put up his camp. It had a good supply of wood. As he was looking for a spot to put his sluice, he could hear two men yelling down at Old Jim's camp. Gold Dust grabbed his rifle and ran down to the corner of the river. He could see Jim on the ground, and a man with a gun kicking him.

Gold Dust ran from one large rock, then over to some smaller rocks, back to some big rocks, then into some willows and over to a large rock 20 feet from Old Jim and the robber. Now what to do?

He could hear the robber yelling at old Jim that he wanted Jim's gold. Old Jim told him to go to hell. Gold Dust was thinking it could be him on the ground looking up at a gun. Then Gold Dust took an aim at the robber as he was kicking poor old Jim. All that Gold Dust could think about was what his daddy told him, "If you have to shoot any animal, shoot it in the chest, it will kill it." Then Gold Dust yelled, "Drop your gun!"

The robber turned and shot at him. Gold Dust shot back. The robber fell to the ground and did not move. Old Jim got up, kicked that robber and yelled, "Don't mess with Gold Dust. He can shoot a fly off the ear of a mule at a hundred yards."

Gold Dust ran over to Jim. "Are you okay, Jim?"

"I am, but he's not. He's not going to rob any more prospectors. He met his maker. I hope he goes to hell."

Old Jim was hard as nails. Old Jim took the robber's boots, hat, gun and socks. Gold Dust had just shot a man and he felt sick to his stomach. Old Jim looked at him and could see that he had never shot anyone before. "Gold Dust, sit down, God will forgive you. Thank you, Gold Dust, you saved my life. That robber killed one man and was going to kill me too. I owe you my life. That robber could have robbed or killed you too."

The two men sat and talked for about an hour. Then Gold Dust asked, "What should we do with the body, Jim?"

"Maybe a bear or a pack of wolves will drag that damn body away before morning."

Gold Dust went back to his camp and had a large drink of whiskey and went to bed. The next morning, after having breakfast, Gold Dust walked down to Old Jim's camp with his shovel to dig a hole to put the robber's body in. When he reached Old Jim's camp, he could see Jim coming up the river with a horse. When Old Jim reached his camp, he looked at Gold Dust and said, "Here's a horse for you. It's that robber's horse. You can use a good horse, Gold Dust."

"No, you can keep the horse, Jim. I don't need a horse. I have my lucky mule, that's all I need."

"Okay, I'll take that damn body to town, maybe there's a reward for him. If there's a reward, I'll bring it back for you. I'll sell the horse, saddle and his guns. It'll be good for a dollar or two."

"That's good. You keep half of the money and give my half to O'Donald, the blacksmith. He'll keep it for me."

"Let's have a look in the saddle bags, Gold Dust."

"Okay, you look, Jim."

"Look, Gold Dust, here's a pocket watch. What does the writing say?"

"Let me see, Jim. Oh my God! It says, 'Paddy O'Donald.' Maybe he's the robber that killed O'Donald's son. If this is the robber that killed

O'Donald's son, maybe he can now put his son to rest knowing that the man that killed his son is dead."

"Give me a hand to tie him to my mule. Tie that damn body tight, I don't want to lose him on my way to town. Gold Dust, can you keep an eye on my claim until I get back in four days?"

"Okay, Jim, I can do that for you. Jim, can you do something for me?"

"Anything you want, Gold Dust."

"Can you take the watch to O'Donald? And let him see the body."

"Consider it done, young man."

"Oh, can you stake a claim for me, when you get to town?"

"Yup, anything you want, Gold Dust."

Jim got on the horse, grabbed the mule's rope and started for town.

Chapter Six

Gold Dust started to work his claim. By the end of the day, he had a small bag of gold dust and 20 small nuggets. It was a good day. He looked for a good place to hide his gold. He found a hole under a big rock. But if someone could see his tracks they might find his gold. What to do? Then he had a good idea. He would use a spot by the rock as his bathroom. No one would go looking for gold in that spot. He went back to his camp and had something to eat. By now it was dark. He grabbed his bottle of whiskey, had one big drink and looked up at the full moon, "God, forgive me for taking the life of a man."

As he sat and looked at the moon and stars, a wolf howled. It made Gold Dust jump. He looked to the top of the riverbank and there was a wolf standing looking down at him. It was beautiful. The wolf howled again. Gold Dust felt calm and sat looking at the wolf on the bank for about an hour. Then he went to bed.

In the morning he went to the river to get water to make coffee. He could see tracks that looked like dog tracks. It was that wolf that made the tracks. He looked up to the bank and that wolf was looking at him. "Maybe this was God's way of saying he forgives me, Paddy."

Gold Dust had breakfast, sat and had coffee and a smoke and then he looked at Paddy. "Well, it's time to move that boulder, Paddy. I need to get under that damn boulder. Five sticks of dynamite should be enough to move it. Yup, I'll just dig a hole under that boulder; put the five sticks in, light the fuse and run." Gold Dust lit the fuse and ran to some rocks about 50 yards away. He stood and looked at that boulder thinking maybe one stick would have been enough.

Then, "BOOM!!"

"Oh, my God, yup, one stick would have been enough, not five!" That boulder went 50 feet in the air and landed in the river. He walked over to the hole and stood looking at it, shaking his head, "Yup, one stick, not five."

"Is that you, Gold Dust? Don't shoot me; I'm a friend of Old Jim's."

"I'm not going to shoot you."

"My name is Tim Buck."

"Good morning, Tim Buck."

"I've got a claim downriver from here. I'm just getting back from town and heard that big bang and saw that boulder go up in the air. How much dynamite did you use?"

"Five sticks, but that was too much. One would have done the job."

"Yup, Gold Dust, one was enough, but you moved that boulder right into the river."

"Yup, I did, Tim Buck."

"Well, I must go back to my claim, Gold Dust. Oh, I have some coffee and whiskey for you from Old Jim."

"Thank you, Tim Buck, maybe I'll walk down to your camp tonight."

"I'll have some beans on for you and coffee."

"Okay, I'll be down after dark."

The two men went on with their day. By the end of the day Gold Dust had a little gold, but it was still a good day. He took his gold and put it in his hiding place. Then he walked to Tim Buck's camp for beans and coffee. He could see the light of Tim

Buck's camp and called out, "It's me, Tim. Those beans smell good."

"Gold Dust, you're just in time. The beans are ready."

"Great, I could eat a horse!"

"Well, I don't have any horsemeat. I have some rabbit in them beans."

"Rabbit will do, Tim."

"Grab a bowl and dig in, Gold Dust."

"Okay."

The two men ate and talked. When they were done eating Tim Buck pulled out a bottle of rum, "Have a drink. It will loosen your tongue, young man."

"Okay, just one, Tim. I have to work hard tomorrow."

"Yup, me too. I guess if I keep drinking rum, I won't get up in the morning."

"Okay, I'm going up to my camp, Tim. Maybe I'll see you in a day or two."

"Have a good night, Gold Dust. Thanks for coming over."

"Thanks for the food and drinks. You have a good night."

Gold Dust walked back to his camp. When he reached his camp, he walked over to Paddy, "Would you like some sugar, Paddy? Have a small piece. You're a lucky mule and a good one. See you in the morning."

Gold Dust walked over and made a fire. The air in the valley was cool at night, and hot all day. As he sat looking up at the stars, he could see the moon coming up over the mountains. It was the most beautiful thing he had ever seen. Then he could hear the wolf howl. He looked up at the river bank, and that wolf was looking at him. The wolf howled again and walked along the top of the bank, then stopped right in front of the moon. This was like stories he read in some books before coming to Canada. Gold Dust sat for about two hours and then went to bed.

In the morning, Gold Dust was up before light. Once he had something to eat, he took Paddy up the bank and over to a small lake. There was some nice grass for Paddy to eat. The air was cool before the sun came up. The cool air kept the bugs from moving around too much. Once the sun came up, the bugs got bad and they went back to the river.

He went to his sluice and started to work. By noon he had five good-sized nuggets and two small bags of gold dust. He had to hide his gold in his hiding place. It was too much gold to keep by his sluice. He was a very happy man. Maybe it was the mother lode or maybe it was just a very good day.

He kept working that hole where he had moved the boulder with the dynamite. By the end of the day, he had a lot of gold. He took his gold and put it into his hiding place. As he made a fire, he was thinking that he was a rich man. Maybe he did have the luck of forty Irishmen, or was it Paddy, the lucky mule? He had something to eat and a good drink of whiskey. Before going to bed, he thanked God for all the gold he had for the day.

The next morning, Gold Dust was up before the crows. When it was light enough he was at the sluice, working hard. By noon the gold was running out. By the end of the day there was very little gold left in the hole. He would have to move the sluice. As he sat by his fire, thinking that he would have to take his gold pan and go look for a good spot to put his sluice, he realized, "I'm a rich man even if I don't find any more gold before I go back to town. Thank you, God."

As he sat in the dark looking at the stars he was thinking of Elephant Mountain. "Is there gold on that mountain? I have to go and look before winter comes."

Chapter Seven

In the morning, he took Paddy to the small lake where there was some good grass for him to eat. As the two of them walked a trail to the little lake, Gold Dust was so happy he was singing and dancing. He looked like a little leprechaun, jumping and dancing.

On his way back to his camp he stopped to have a look at Old Jim's camp. Jim's camp looked okay. When he got back to his camp, he grabbed his gold pan and walked to the river. He began panning along the river and looked for a good spot to put his sluice. After about one hour he could see someone coming up the river, it looked like it could be Old Jim and his mule. When they reached him, it was Old Jim and his mule.

Old Jim called out, "Good morning, Gold Dust."

"Good morning, Jim. It's a really good morning!"

"You must have found some gold, young man."

"How did you know, Jim?"

"You have a smile from ear to ear, and it's like you're walking on air."

"I did find some gold, but it ran out."

"You have to keep looking up and down the river, Gold Dust."

"Okay, Jim."

"Gold Dust, give me a hand to get some coffee happening."

"I'll go and get some water, Jim. You can get the fire going."

"Boy, I have a story to tell you, Gold Dust. I'll tell you when you get back with the water."

"Okay, here's the water."

"Here, you're going to need this drink, Gold Dust."

"Okay, Jim."

"Well, it's like this. That robber was the one that killed O'Donald's son. The sheriff said he killed five men that there was a reward for, but maybe there were more he had killed."

"Was the watch O'Donald's?"

"Yup, it was his dad's. O'Donald began crying. I had to go to the jail to get the reward from the sheriff or I was going to cry."

"What was the reward for that damn robber?"

"Four hundred dollars and I got one hundred for the horse, saddle and guns. I gave O'Donald your half."

"Thanks, Jim. Did you stake a claim for me?"

"Yup, it starts at my stake and goes up to the next corner and a hundred yards back on each side."

"Thanks for doing that for me."

"No problem, Gold Dust. The sheriff would like you to talk to him when you get to town."

"Okay, Jim. I met Tim Buck."

"Tim Buck's a good man, Gold Dust."

"Yes, he is. I went down to his camp one night for something to eat and to bullshit."

"He bullshits, Gold Dust, but not as good as me."

The two men sat and had a good bullshit. After three hours, Gold Dust had enough.

"Jim, there is so much bullshit here I'm going to need a shovel to shovel my way out of your camp!"

The two men laughed and laughed. Then Gold Dust went back to his camp and grabbed his gold pan. He walked up to the top corner of the river to put in his stake. Then he began panning for gold. He worked his way down the river and marked the spots where he found gold. By the time he reached his camp, he had marked 20 spots and had 30 gold nuggets. Most of them were small, but some of them had a little size to them. He had enough gold for the day.

Then he went back to his camp. He sat and had a coffee and something to eat. He sat thinking of O'Donald and the robber that killed his son. He began to get sad. Then Paddy walked over and pushed him with his nose. "What do you want Paddy? You want to go to that little lake, don't you? Let me grab my rifle."

Paddy and Gold Dust walked up to the little lake. When they reached the lake, Gold Dust found a good spot to sit by a big rock. Paddy walked and ate grass by the lake. It was a hot day; the heat kept the bugs down. Gold Dust sat thinking of Elephant Mountain and how to get to the top to look for gold. He was not sad anymore as he watched Paddy playing with the ground squirrels. "Maybe I can shoot a rabbit and make a stew. That's what I'm going to do."

Gold Dust got up and grabbed his rifle and called for Paddy to come with him. Gold Dust walked to a small stand of trees. Paddy came running up behind him. He and Paddy walked into the trees. He could see rabbit droppings. Gold Dust sat on a rock and let Paddy walk around. Then out came a rabbit. It ran over to a small rock looking at Paddy. Gold Dust shot, the rabbit fell to the ground.

"I got him Paddy."

Poor Paddy didn't know that Gold Dust was going to shoot his rifle. Paddy ran into the trees. "Come back, it's okay!" Gold Dust ran after him but he could not keep up with him. Gold Dust went back, grabbed the rabbit and started back to his camp. He kept calling for Paddy but he could not see him anywhere. When he got back to camp there was Paddy. "Paddy, you're one brave mule. You ran so fast that the bugs could not keep up with you! That's okay; you're my lucky mule, Paddy. Here have some sugar, you're a good mule."

Gold Dust cleaned the rabbit and put it in a pot. He dug out some potatoes and carrots and got them ready for the stew. Paddy came over to try and get a carrot. Gold Dust laughed at him, "Here, Paddy, you can have one."

He put the pot over the fire. Then Gold Dust went back to his sluice and began moving it upriver. By dark, he had the sluice moved to his new spot. When he got back to camp, he pulled the stew off the fire and put some coffee on. That stew smelled good and he dished up a plate. It didn't take him long to eat one plate, then he had one more. Moving that sluice had made him one hungry man. He thanked God for his day and went to bed.

About three in the morning, Paddy woke Gold Dust up. "What is it Paddy? What do you smell or do you hear something?" Paddy was not a happy mule something was upsetting him. The moon was high in the night sky. Gold Dust could see a little. "It's okay, Paddy."

Gold Dust grabbed his Colt 45. He walked away from his camp. As he looked up the river, he could see something, but he didn't know what it was. It was moving down the river, but slowly. When it got close enough to see what it was, he looked at his Colt 45 and then at Paddy. "I'm going to need a bigger gun, Paddy, it's a grizzly."

Gold Dust and Paddy walked back to the camp. He grabbed his rifle and walked away from his camp so he could see the grizzly. Paddy came and stood beside him. That big old bear stopped and looked at them, then kept walking down the river. Gold Dust and Paddy walked back to camp. It was about four in the morning. He stayed up and had something to eat. Then he walked up to his sluice, and Paddy came with him. The sun would be up around six.

Gold Dust started moving sand over to the sluice before it was light. When the sun came up, he had a good pile of sand by the sluice. By noon he had some small gold nuggets and some dust. By the end of the day he did okay, not a lot, but some. By the end of week four it was time to go back to town. Gold Dust had a very good month. He put his gold in his saddlebags and went down to Old Jim's camp. "Morning, Jim, I'm going back to town. Do you need anything? I'll be back in four or five days."

"I do, I need some coffee and rum, maybe some smoke, a little chew and some beef jerky. That will do me."

"I have some coffee you can have, Jim."

"Great, I'm out of coffee. That's the last in the pot. Do you need some money Gold Dust?"

"No, Jim, I'll see you when I get back." The two men said goodbye, and Gold Dust started his walk back to Nelson.

Chapter Eight

He was looking at the beauty of the valley. Then out of a stand of trees about one hundred yards from them a wolf walked out. "Look, Paddy, there's a wolf over there. Maybe that's the wolf that came by the camp." That wolf walked with them until he reached the trail that went up to the pass. There the wolf stopped. He looked at them, then turned and walked back towards the valley. Paddy and Gold Dust started up the trail for the pass.

By noon they had made the top of the pass. They stopped for about an hour. Gold Dust gave Paddy some oats and he had something to eat. Then it was time to move on. "Come on Paddy. We have to get across the pass by dark." The sun was hot, but the air was cool. Winter was in the air.

By dark they had made the far end of the pass. "This looks like a good spot to make camp for the night, Paddy." There was no wood to make a fire but this would be okay for one night. By two in the morning it was cold. There was a frost on the ground. It was too cold for Gold Dust to sleep. He got up and packed up camp, "Come on, Paddy, it's too damn cold up here to sleep." The moon was high in the night sky. He could see enough that they could walk on the trail to get down off the pass to where there was some wood to make a fire. By four they had made it down to a spot that had some firewood. Gold Dust made a fire; put a blanket over Paddy and one around himself. It was warmer with a fire and he went to sleep.

In the morning Gold Dust made some coffee and something to eat. As he sat drinking a coffee, he could hear someone coming up the trail. He got up and grabbed his rifle. He didn't want to get robbed. He had too much gold to have it robbed. Then he could see an old prospector with a mule.

"Morning, young man, they call me Mad Dog."

"I'm Gold Dust."

"You're the man that killed that damn robber that old Jim came to town with."

"Yup, that's me."

"Jim told me at the saloon that when you shot that damn robber he was a hundred yards away and it was almost dark."

"No, I was 20 feet from him and it was light."

46

"Jim told me you would say that."

"Well, Mad Dog, you know Jim can pile the bullshit pretty high."

The two men laughed. "That he can, Gold Dust. Do you have any coffee in that pot?"

"I do, Mad Dog, would you like some?"

"That will be great. There was a man looking for you in town last week. He was the brother of that robber you shot."

"He was looking for me?"

"Yup, he went over to O'Donald's shop and asked if he knew where you were. O'Donald asked him, 'What do you want him for?' He told O'Donald, 'He shot my brother, and when I find him I'm going to kill him.' O'Donald told him that his brother shot his son six years ago. He said, 'Too bad for him; tell someone who gives a shit!'

O'Donald had seen this man's picture on the wall of the jail. O'Donald grabbed the man and threw him to the ground. He tied his hands and asked him if he was ready to meet his maker. O'Donald told him he was not going to take another son from him. Then O'Donald told him to kiss his ass goodbye. He shot him in the head with his own gun, just like his

47

son was shot with his hands tied behind his back. He killed that man so he wouldn't kill you."

"My God, Mad Dog, he shot him, so he wouldn't come after me. I'm like a son to him."

"That he did, Gold Dust."

"Well, Mad Dog, I have to pack up camp, and make it to town before dark."

"Thanks for the coffee, I'll see you around."

"Okay, Mad Dog."

As Gold Dust walked down the trail he was thinking of what Mad Dog had said about O'Donald. Gold Dust thought, "He's like a dad to me. I will pay his way back to Ireland when he is ready to go. I'm going to be a rich man when I get to town."

By noon he had made good time. It was getting warmer as he walked down the trail. By three he could see Elephant Mountain. One more hour and he would be in town.

As he walked down the hill into town, he looked up at the mountain, "Could there be some gold on that mountain? Why do I keep looking at it and dreaming of it?"

Chapter Nine

As he walked down the street, people said hi to him. Prospectors stopped and shook his hand, and thanked him for shooting that robber. As he walked over to O'Donald's shop, the sheriff stopped him. "I'm Sheriff Bob, and you're Gold Dust?"

"Yes, I am. What can I do for you?"

"You think you could come and see me before you go back in the hills?"

"I can do that, Sheriff."

"Thanks, Gold Dust."

Gold Dust walked over to the blacksmith shop. There was O'Donald with a bottle of whiskey. "Come over here, Gold Dust. Let's have a talk and a drink."

"That sounds good to me, O'Donald."

"A lot has happened in the last month to the two of us."

"That it has, O'Donald. That it has."

The two men sat and talked for a bit. Then it was time for Gold Dust to go and sell his gold.

"I'll put a fire under the tub for you. It should be ready when you get back."

49

"You don't have to do that for me, O'Donald."

"It makes me happy."

"If it makes you happy, do it."

Gold Dust grabbed his saddlebag and went to sell his gold. O'Donald lit a fire under the tub and gave Paddy some hay and looked at his shoes. When Gold Dust got back, he had a big smile and was singing.

"You found some gold, young man."

"I did. How did you know?"

"Well, it looks like you're walking on air, and you're singing. That means you found a woman in the bank or you found some gold." The two men had a good laugh. "Now get in that tub; you smell like that mule."

"Okay."

"I'll see you at the saloon."

"I'm going to be a bit. I'm going to buy some new clothes."

"Okay, I'll see you when you get there."

O'Donald walked over to the saloon and sat down. Lucky and Happy came over to talk to him. Gold Dust had his bath, went over to the store and bought some new clothes, new boots and a new hat. Then he went back to the shop and put his new clothes on, thinking, "They will love me tonight." He walked over to the saloon.

When he walked in, everyone looked at him. Some of the prospectors came over and shook his hand and bought him some drinks. Then he went over to O'Donald's table. "I like your whoring clothes, Gold Dust. They look good on you."

"Thanks, maybe I'll get lucky tonight."

"Would you like me to get her to come over here for you?"

The two men had a good laugh.

"No, she stole my money the last time I was here. That's not lucky."

"Well, those girls need to make a living too."

The two men drank and played cards. The girls were having fun with Gold Dust and O'Donald. By midnight, O'Donald had to go back to his shop. He had work to do for the silver mine. Gold Dust stayed for the night at the saloon.

In the morning Gold Dust walked to the jail to talk to Sheriff Bob. When he was done, he went over to the blacksmith shop to see O'Donald. "Morning, young man, did you have enough to drink last night?"

"That I did. My legs are weak."

"Go and get something to eat over at the hotel. They have good food."

"I'll do that. I'm a little hungry from all that work last night. Are you coming over with me, O'Donald?"

"No, I have too much work to do."

"Okay, I'll see you."

Gold Dust walked over to the hotel. He had something to eat and got a room. He was going to sleep for most of the day. He walked back over to O'Donald's shop to give Paddy some oats and hay. "O'Donald, will you take care of Paddy tonight? I got a room at the hotel to catch up on my sleep."

"Okay, Gold Dust you have a good sleep. I'll see you later."

Gold Dust went back to the hotel. When he went inside there was a young woman standing at the desk. She was the most beautiful woman he had ever seen. She had long hair and a beautiful smile. His legs got weak. Gold Dust fell in love. "Good morning. My name is Gold Dust."

"My name's Lizzie. I cook here at the hotel."

"I'm a prospector."

"You're the man who shot the robber that shot O'Donald's son and five men and maybe more."

"I had to shoot him. He was going to shoot Old Jim."

"Are you staying in the hotel?"

"I'm here for one day. I have a spot at O'Donald's shop to sleep."

"Okay, Gold Dust, I have to go back to work now. What is your real name?"

"Paddy."

"Maybe we can talk again some time, Paddy."

"That would be nice, Lizzie."

Gold Dust went up to his room and went to sleep. He didn't get up until the next morning. When he got up, he walked over to O'Donald's shop.

"Morning, Gold Dust, you had a long sleep."

"I did, I must have needed that sleep."

"Come in the shop, I have something for you to see."

"Okay, what do you have for me to see?"

"Here, I built a room on the back of the shop for you with some old lumber I had laying around here."

"Thank you, O'Donald. I have to pay you for building that room."

"I told you before. When you get rich, you can pay me back with a one way ticket back to Ireland."

"When do you want to go back, O'Donald?"

O'Donald laughed, "You're not rich enough yet, Gold Dust."

"Maybe I am."

"I'll let you know when I'm ready."

"Okay."

"You'll have to buy a stove and some pipe for that room."

"I'll go and see if I can get a stove at the store."

"I have that reward money for you, Gold Dust."

"You keep it, O'Donald, I don't need it now."

"I'll keep it for you."

"Okay, O'Donald. I met the most beautiful young woman at the hotel. Her name's Lizzie. I'm in love."

"Lizzie would make you a good wife. She can cook a good meal."

"A good wife? That's a little too soon, O'Donald."

The two men had a little laugh.

"I'll have a look at Paddy's shoes when you're gone for the stove."

"See you when I get back."

Chapter Ten

Gold Dust was walking over to the store. He heard someone call out, "Paddy, how are you today?" He turned and there she was, smiling at him. He grinned shyly, "Good, Lizzie. And you?"

"I'm very good today."

"Can I walk with you?"

"I would like that, Paddy."

Gold Dust and Lizzie walked over to the store. Gold Dust looked for a stove and Lizzie bought some food. Gold Dust had to wait for a stove to come in on the paddleboat in two days. When the two lovebirds left the store, Gold Dust looked at her, "Would you like me to carry your bags?"

"Yes, that would be nice, Paddy. You're a long ways from home. Do you have a lady back in Ireland?"

"No, Lizzie, no lady back home."

"I'm going to have a picnic this afternoon down at the river. Would you like to come with me?"

"I'd love to, Lizzie."

The lovebirds walked past O'Donald's shop. He waved at them and smiled. Gold Dust and Lizzie walked to the end of town to Lizzie's house. "Thank you, I'll see you at one, Paddy."

"Okay, at one." Gold Dust walked back to O'Donald's shop.

As he came up to the shop O'Donald smiled, "You're in love. I can see it in your eyes, young man."

"I am! She's beautiful. We're going for a picnic at one."

"Don't let, you know what, do the talking."

"I won't."

"Let your heart do the talking, young man."

"She makes me feel good all over and she's beautiful."

"She is, Gold Dust. Her dad died up at the silver mine about five years ago. Her mom died two years ago of pneumonia. Young man, you be nice to her. She's been hurt enough."

"She didn't tell me. I'll be a gentleman, O'Donald."

"You better be or I'll whop your ass - and you know I can!"

"Okay, dad, I'll be nice."

The two men had a laugh. Then O'Donald lit some wood under the tub, "Okay, young man, get your ass in this tub. You don't want to smell like the saloon."

"Okay, okay, now you sound like my mom."

Gold Dust had his bath then sat and talked with O'Donald. The two men had some laughs and talked about how to be nice to women, what to say and how to say it. Now Gold Dust was ready to go and see Lizzie. As he walked over to Lizzie's house, it was like everyone in town was looking at him. He was getting nervous - the closer he got the more nervous he got. By the time he got to her door he was a mess. He knocked on the door. He could hear her coming to the door. Then it opened... "Come in, Paddy."

"Thank you, Lizzie."

"Would you like a whiskey?"

"Yes, that would be nice."

"Relax, Paddy, I'm not going to bite you."

"I know, Lizzie. I'm a little nervous."

"Me too, but we are adults. You must be the same age as me, Paddy."

"I'm twenty. I'll be twenty-one in three months."

"I'll be twenty-one in four months."

"We are the same age, Lizzie."

The two lovebirds sat and talked for a bit. Then they walked down to the river to have their picnic. As Lizzie unpacked the picnic lunch Gold Dust could not stop talking. Lizzie smiled at him as he talked. Then she pulled out a bottle of whiskey. Gold Dust stopped talking and looked at the whiskey, "A bottle of whiskey can stop a man from talking - but after three or four drinks he starts talking again."

The two lovebirds laughed. Then they had a drink and something to eat. They played along the riverbank. It was like two kids playing games. Then it was time to go back to town. On the walk back Lizzie grabbed his hand. He smiled at her and she smiled back at him. The two lovebirds walked hand and hand to Lizzie's house. "Thank you, Paddy, I had a great day."

"I had a great day too."

"Would you like to come for dinner?"

"I'd love to, Lizzie."

"Okay, I'll see you at six."

Then Lizzie gave him a kiss on the cheek and ran into the house. Gold Dust's face turned red.

Then he walked over to O'Donald's shop. When he reached the shop, O'Donald began laughing, "Young man, you're really in love. I can see it in your eyes and in your face."

"I'm in love. She kissed me on the cheek."

"I can see a wife in the makings, Gold Dust."

"She's the same age as me."

"That's good, Gold Dust. I wouldn't want you to marry an older woman."

"I'm not talking marriage. I'm talking of having fun. She's fun to be around and she makes me feel good."

"Okay, I'm just having fun with you. When her mom died, I helped her get through her hard times."

"She didn't tell me that you helped her."

"You're not married yet, Gold Dust. She doesn't have to tell you everything about herself."

"I know, but I want to know everything about her, O'Donald."

"Slow down, Gold Dust, give her time. If you move too fast you might scare her away. She must like you. You're the first young man that I've seen her with, but there are not too many young men in this town."

"I know, O'Donald."

"Will you get ready, Gold Dust? Maybe you could have a shave."

"Maybe I'll go and get a haircut before going over to Lizzie's. What do you think O'Donald?"

"That's a good idea, young man."

"Okay, O'Donald, I'll go and get a shave and a haircut."

"I'm going to the saloon. I'll see you later."

Gold Dust walked over to the barber shop. When he was getting his shave the barber told him, "Someone found some gold in the next valley and a lot of prospectors are going over to the valley."

When he was done at the barber shop Gold Dust went to talk to O'Donald in the saloon. When he walked into the saloon, O'Donald was sitting in his corner drinking a whiskey. "Gold Dust, come and sit down, we have to talk."

"Okay."

"Did you hear that someone found a lot of gold in the next valley?"

"I did, when I was over at the barber shop, O'Donald."

"You should go back to your claim in the morning, Gold Dust. You'll have prospectors all over your claim. You should go and get your supplies before you go to Lizzie's."

"Okay, O'Donald, I'll go and get them now. Could you have a look at Paddy for me?"

"Okay, you go now. Say hi to Lizzie for me when you go over to her place."

"I will." Gold Dust went and picked up his supplies and then began walking over to Lizzie's house for dinner. The closer he got, the faster he walked. As he walked up the stairs he could see Lizzie looking out the window. She smiled at him and ran to open the door.

"Come in, Paddy, and have a seat. Dinner will be ready soon."

"Okay, Lizzie, I could eat a horse."

"I didn't cook horse, but I did cook a chicken. Will that do?"

"I didn't mean I wanted you to cook a horse. I meant I was as hungry as one."

"I know what you meant, Paddy. Let's have something to drink before dinner. It looks like you need one."

"That sounds good. I do need one, Lizzie."

"Relax, Paddy, did O'Donald tell you to be nice to me or he would kick your ass."

"He did, Lizzie."

"I'll talk to him and maybe I'll kick his ass." The two love birds laughed. Gold Dust told Lizzie that he was going back to the valley in the morning. Lizzie told Gold Dust she would come and see him off in the morning. After a good dinner and some laughs Gold Dust had to go and get some sleep. Lizzie walked him to the door.

"I'll see you in the morning, Paddy." Then she gave him a kiss on the cheek and ran into the house.

Gold Dust was in love. As he walked back to the blacksmith shop, he was thinking that Lizzie would make a good wife.

Chapter Eleven

When he reached the shop, O'Donald was sitting on some hay in the shop. "How was your dinner with Lizzie?"

"It was good, O'Donald."

"Paddy is ready for tomorrow, but you don't seem to be."

"No, I'm not. That damn love bug has me wanting to stay."

"Young man, that's okay. You're only human; she is a beautiful woman. I would feel the same if it was me."

"I know, but I'd like to stay for a day or two more."

"She will be here when you get back, young man."

"I'm going to bed now. I'll see you in the morning, O'Donald."

"Okay, you have a good sleep."

In the morning the two men were up before the crows. By light they had Paddy ready to go. The two men sat and talked. O'Donald told him about a cave. "There is a cave at the bottom of the pass. It's a place to put up camp for the night before going over the pass."

"Okay, I'll find it."

"Gold Dust, you'll have to keep an eye on the tops of the mountains for snow. If it snows too much, you won't get over the pass and it looks like it's going to snow soon."

"Okay, I'll keep a good eye on the tops of the mountains."

"I hope you do, Gold Dust. Last year four prospectors froze on the top of the pass. They got caught in a wind and snowstorm."

"What if I get caught in the valley, where do I go?"

"You can wait for a good warm day and try to make it over in one day or you can go to the next town, but it's a five day walk."

"That's a long walk."

"That pass may be open. It's not as high but it takes about three days to get over it."

"I really don't want to go to the next valley."

"You'll have to bring some wood to make a fire if you go that way and leave everything you don't need behind. It can be a very hard walk. You'll have to trust your gut feeling on that one, Gold Dust."

"Thanks, O'Donald."

"Well, young man, are you ready to go or are you too much in love?"

"I am in love. She's a beautiful woman. And I know I have to go back to my claim."

"Talking about a woman, here she comes, Gold Dust."

"Good morning, you two."

"Morning, Lizzie."

"I have some jam and some bread for you, Paddy."

"Thanks, Lizzie."

"I'll let you two lovebirds be. I'll see you when you get back, Gold Dust, or should I call you Paddy?"

"I'll see you when I get back, O'Donald."

"Okay, I've got work to do."

"Should I be calling you Gold Dust, Paddy?"

"No, Lizzie, you can call me Paddy."

"Okay, will you be coming by when you get back?"

"If you would like me to I will."

"I'd like that, Paddy."

"Okay, I have to go now, Lizzie. I'll see you when I get back."

Lizzie gave him a hug and a kiss and ran into O'Donald's shop. Gold Dust walked down the street to the end of town and up the hill to the trail that went to the pass. He stopped when he reached the top of the hill and turned and looked at the little town of Nelson and Elephant Mountain. It would be about one month before he would see them again. "That damn mountain is looking at me again, Paddy. There has to be gold up on that mountain. We have to look when we get back before winter sets in."

Chapter Twelve

The two walked all day and didn't see anyone on the trail. It began raining around noon. It was a cold rain. When they reached the bottom of the pass, Gold Dust looked for and found the cave. "Here it is Paddy. It's big enough for you to come into. Let's go and get some wood for the night. Come on, Paddy, don't just stand there looking at me." Paddy was not going to move. He just stood in the entrance of the cave and looked at Gold Dust.

"Well, you stay and I'll go and get some wood. I don't blame you, not wanting to come out here in the wet and cold. If I were you, I would stay in that cave too." Gold Dust went and got wood for the night, as Paddy looked at him from inside the cave. Gold Dust just laughed at Paddy every time he came in with some wood. When he had enough wood in the cave, he made a fire with some dry wood that was in the cave. "It's big enough and has a hole in the top to let the smoke out, Paddy."

As he sat with a coffee, he was thinking of Lizzie. If it snowed would he get back to town? It was warm in the cave. Then Paddy went out of the cave into the rain. "Where are you going, Paddy? Come back here." Paddy kept walking; then he stopped. "That's where you're going. A mule that's house trained. What's next, Paddy, are you going to talk to me?" Gold Dust had a good laugh and began making something to eat. Then he heard someone outside the cave. He grabbed his rifle and walked to the entrance.

"Can I come in out of the cold, young man?"

"Come on in. Bring that mule in here he looks as cold as you."

"They call me Mud Slide."

"I'm Gold Dust."

"Are you the one that shot that robber?"

"That's me."

"Old Jim told me about you shooting him from two hundred yards just before dark."

"It was twenty feet and it was light out."

"Old Jim said you would say that. You think I could have some of that coffee?"

"Help yourself, Mud Slide."

"Are you going over the pass, Gold Dust?"

"I am. Mud Slide, did you just come down the pass?"

"I did and it was snowing and cold. If it keeps snowing you won't get over the pass in the morning."

The two men sat and talked for about two hours before they lay down to sleep. It stopped raining around ten; maybe it would be okay to go over the pass in the morning. Gold Dust was up before the crows. He had coffee and something to eat. It was going to be a long day. "Okay, Mud Slide, I'll see you around. I have to get over the pass before dark."

"You be careful going over the pass. If there is too much snow come back down and try tomorrow."

"Okay, Mud Slide, I'll do that."

Gold Dust began his trek up to the pass. The higher he trekked the more snow there was. By the time he made the top of the pass it was very cold, but the sun was warm. He had to make it across the top of the pass and down to the valley. When he got halfway across the top, it began blowing the snow around and made it cold as hell. Gold Dust let Paddy go first and he walked behind him. When they reached the other side of the pass and started down, Gold Dust thanked Paddy for getting them across the pass. When they reached the bottom of the pass, they stopped.

Gold Dust made a fire and put on some coffee. He gave Paddy some oats, took off his packs and let him walk around. It was warmer at the bottom of the pass and Gold Dust would make camp here for the night. He had three hours of light left, but it had been a long hard day for the two of them. He sat up next to his pack and fell to sleep.

He woke up to the sound of someone yelling at their mule. He looked down the trail and there was an old prospector pulling on his mule. He was a little mad at his mule. Gold Dust laughed and walked down with Paddy to see if they could help. "Good afternoon. Do you want a hand with that mule? I'm Gold Dust."

"I could use four hands with this damn mule. They call me Big Foot. You can tell why. If you had feet like this you wouldn't need snowshoes to go over the pass. Did you say your name was Gold Dust?"

"I did."

"You're the one that shot that damn robber. He robbed me about four months ago and took some of my gold. He couldn't find it all. I had most of it in the toes of my boots. Lucky for me he didn't want my boots. They were too damn big for him."

"It pays to have big feet, Big Foot."

"That it does, Gold Dust."

"Let me try to get your mule to move. What's the mule's name?"

"Shit Head."

"That's a different kind of name for a mule. Come on, Shit Head, let's go up to my camp."

Shit Head began walking with Gold Dust up the trail to his camp. "I don't believe this. I've been pulling and pushing that damn mule all day and you talk to him and he goes with you."

"Are you going over the pass tonight, Big Foot?"

"No, not till in the morning. Did you come over today?"

"I did and it was cold and the wind was blowing hard."

"You think I could make camp here with you for the night, Gold Dust?"

"That would be okay, Big Foot."

"Can I have some of your coffee, young man?"

"Help yourself, maybe you would like some whiskey to go in that coffee?"

"That, I'd like. Old Jim told me you were a good man and you are."

The two men talked and laughed for a few hours then went to sleep. In the morning the two men ate and drank coffee. Then it was time to go on their way. "You be careful going over the top of that pass. There's about a foot of snow up there, Big Foot."

"I'll be okay. Thanks for letting me stay at your camp, Gold Dust."

Gold Dust went down into the valley and Big Foot went up to the pass. As he walked to the valley, he looked up at the top of the mountains covered with snow. Maybe he should have gone back to town, but it was too late now. It might warm up before he had to go back. It was beautiful in the valley but if it snowed too much on the pass he would be trapped on this side of the pass and it could be spring before he could get back to Nelson.

Chapter Thirteen

When Gold Dust and Paddy reached the trail that turned north, they stopped and had a break before going on. As Gold Dust sat on a log having a smoke, something ran behind a rock about two hundred yards north of him. As he looked, out came that wolf and it looked at him. Then it began catching mice. It was beautiful to watch him hunt for mice.

"Well it's time to go, Paddy. We'll be at camp soon and you won't have to do anything but eat and sleep all day."

When they reached Old Jim's camp, he was sitting having a coffee. Gold Dust called out to him, "Morning, Jim, you have some coffee in that pot?"

"Grab a cup. I just made it, Gold Dust."

"I've got your supplies, Jim."

"Thanks, young man. There have been a lot of prospectors coming through here in the last few days. They said that someone found a lot of gold somewhere around here."

"I heard in town that it was a lot of gold, Jim."

73

"I had to chase some of those prospectors off your claim. They were like flies on the back of a mule."

"Thanks, Jim. You're a good man."

"Gold Dust, how much snow was there on the pass?"

"About a foot, Jim, it was blowing hard. It was a long hard trek across the top of the pass."

"Well, Gold Dust, we need to keep a close eye on that mountain over there. When the snow gets down to the tree line, it will be time to go back to Nelson."

"Okay, Jim, I'll keep a close eye. What if the snow goes below the tree line?"

"We may not get over the pass. Then we could wait for the snow to melt some or go to the town in the next valley for the winter. That pass is a little lower than this one."

"I don't want to spend the winter in the next town. I have a young woman to get back to in Nelson."

"Do you mean Lucky or is it Happy?"

"No, Jim."

"Who's the lucky woman?"

"It's Lizzie."

"Lizzie! You hound dog, you. She's a beautiful young woman that needs to get married."

"You sound like O'Donald."

"You're one lucky man, Gold Dust."

"Thanks, Jim, do you think we will get the month in before it snows too much?"

"I don't know, Gold Dust, winter's in the air, maybe two or three weeks."

"Okay, I'm going up to my camp, Jim."

"I'll see you later, Gold Dust."

Gold Dust walked up to his camp and took the packs off Paddy and let him roam around. Then he made a fire, put on some coffee and some food. Once he was done eating, he went down to his sluice. The river had risen two feet from the rain and snow. It was flowing faster. The water was cold as ice. As Paddy ventured close to the river Gold Dust laughed, "Paddy, that water is too cold to go swimming in now." Gold Dust went to work but kept thinking of Lizzie, and that Elephant Mountain. "That mountain is real close to Nelson and Lizzie."

Gold Dust stopped early so he could get a good sleep, but he had a good day of gold. As he walked back to his camp, he looked around for Paddy. He was nowhere to be seen. He called and called, but no Paddy. "Maybe he's down at Old Jim's camp?" he wondered. "I'll go down and have a look." He grabbed his rifle and walked down to Old Jim's. "Jim, have you seen Paddy around here?"

"No, I haven't. Did you lose that mule?"

"I did, Jim. I was working. When I walked back to my camp, I couldn't see him."

"Maybe he's at the little lake eating grass or he went back to Nelson."

"I'll go and look up at the little lake. You really don't think he went back to town, do you?"

"Well, I wouldn't put it past him to go back to town. I'll come with you. I need a good walk."

"Thanks, Jim."

The two men walked back up to a little trail. As they walked along, they talked about the river and how if it rained too much they would have to leave. Then something caught Old Jim's eye. "Look, Gold Dust. It's a wolf, why is he standing looking at us? Maybe he ate your mule, shoot him." "No, Jim, he didn't eat my mule and I'm not going to shoot him."

"How do you know he didn't eat your mule?"

"He's a good wolf, Jim. I've seen him around my camp and he came out to the bottom of the pass when I went out."

"He's a big wolf, Gold Dust."

"Look, Jim, there's Paddy over by that big rock. Come here, Paddy, I've been looking for you, you crazy mule."

"Look, Gold Dust, that wolf is really close now. Man he's big but he's a beauty."

"That he is, Jim. Come on, I want to get to sleep early tonight it's been a long day. I have to work hard tomorrow."

"I have to do some work too if I want to eat this winter."

Chapter Fourteen

The two men and Paddy walked back to the river. They reached the top of the bank above Old Jim's camp and there was a man digging in Old Jim's pack. "I know him, Gold Dust. They call him, Bucksaw. Shoot him in the leg. Bucksaw knows that's my camp. What an asshole he is!"

"I can't shoot him in the leg, you know this man."

"Well, if you don't shoot him in the leg, I'll kill him when I get down there."

"Okay, Jim! I'll shoot him in the leg."

"Wait until my pack is out of way of your shot. I don't want a hole in it."

Gold Dust took aim, then shot.

"You got him, Gold Dust. He dropped to the ground like mule shit."

"Should we go down and help him, Jim?"

"Hell no! Listen to him whine, and look at him roll around."

"Maybe we should go down there now, Jim."

"He's okay. Give me your rifle. I want to put some more shots around Bucksaw to make him jump. Maybe he'll get on his mule and go back to town. He will have a good story to tell everyone in the saloon." Old Jim shot around Bucksaw.

He got on his mule and rode out of Old Jim's camp. The two men had a real good laugh and walked down the bank to Jim's camp.

"That was a good shot, Gold Dust. I don't think you hit any bones, but Bucksaw did bleed a lot."

"Maybe we should go find him and stop the bleeding."

"Hell no, he'll put something over the hole in his leg to stop the bleeding."

"Okay, Jim, if you say so."

"Well, he didn't get my rum. Let's have a good drink."

"A drink sounds good, Jim."

After having a drink Gold Dust went back to his camp and put some food on the fire. As he sat and ate, he was thinking of Lizzie and how good she made him feel. Then he grabbed his bottle of whiskey, had a good drink and gazed at the stars. He thanked God for the gold he got that day and went to bed.

When Gold Dust got up in the morning there was a heavy frost that covered the ground. He made a fire and put some coffee on and walked down to his sluice. When he reached his sluice, he could see that the river had risen a foot more. He walked back to his camp and put some coffee in his cup and looked at the mountains. As he gazed at the mountain tops, he was thinking of Elephant Mountain and that he would go and look for gold on that mountain before the winter sat in. He made some breakfast then went to work.

By noon the clouds moved in and it began raining. Gold Dust looked up at the mountains and could see that it was snowing up on the tops. He went back to his camp for some lunch and to warm up by the fire. As he sat drinking a coffee looking down the river, he could see someone walking. As he got closer, Gold Dust could see it was Old Jim. "What's up, Jim?"

"We need to move our camps across the river before the water gets too high to cross."

"Do we need to move them now?"

"That we do, young man. With all that snow on the mountains and this rain, the river will rise fast.

We don't want to get caught on this side. If we do it will take two days for us to get to a spot to cross."

"I'll pack up camp now, Jim."

"Good man, I'll be waiting for you at my camp."

"Okay, Jim."

Gold Dust began packing up his camp. He put his gear on Paddy. Then he took his sluice down and put it up by the bank of the river. The river had risen a foot more. He would have to come back for his sluice. It would be too heavy for Paddy to carry all the gear and the sluice. As Gold Dust and Paddy walked down to Old Jim's camp, the wind began blowing and it was a cold north wind. Old Jim was ready.

"Okay, Jim, let's go across that damn river."

"We have to wait for Tim Buck. He should be here soon."

"There he is, Jim. You know that river came up a foot from this morning?"

"That it did, Gold Dust. Get your slow ass up here, Tim Buck."

"Okay, Jim, I'm going as fast as I can, you old fool."

Just then they could hear a rumble coming from the mountains.

"That's the snow on the mountains sliding down to the river. If we don't get across now we won't get across at all."

"Okay, Jim, let's go across now. Tim Buck, come on."

"Okay, Gold Dust, I'll be right behind you."

The three men began trudging across the river. The flow of the river was strong and it was very hard walking.

"Keep a good hold on that rope, Gold Dust. You don't want to go down the river. You'll be a goner if you do."

"I will, Jim! This water is really cold, Tim."

"You think this is cold, wait until it gets your balls, young man."

"Is it going to get deeper, Tim Buck?" "It's going to get up to your belly button, Gold Dust, and it will be cold as hell."

"Thanks, Tim Buck, I needed to know that."

"Okay, you two; keep moving."

"We will, Jim."

The three men trudged across that ice cold river. When they got up on the river bank they made a large fire and took their wet clothes off.

"I guess we wouldn't make any women happy now, would we? I can't find it, that damn water was too cold."

"That it was, Jim."

The three men had a good laugh and put on some dry clothes, and took the packs off the mules. Old Jim had a tent that they put up and put his small stove in and lit a fire. They stood looking at the river from inside the tent.

"Well we got across just in time, you two." "We did, Jim, are you going to stay here?"

"I think I'm going to, Gold Dust."

"If you stay, I will, Jim."

"What about you, Tim Buck?"

"I think I'm going to go back to town, Jim."

The three men warmed up in the tent for about an hour. By then the water in the river began flowing really fast. As they stood looking at the river, some trees came floating down. The river came up about five feet. The three men had made it across just in time.

Tim Buck began putting his packs on his mule. "Well, you two, I'm going to the bottom of the pass and make camp for the night. I'll go over in the morning."

"We'll see you in town, Tim. Good luck going over the pass."

"Thanks, you two. I'll need some luck." Tim Buck left for the pass.

Chapter Fifteen

Gold Dust and Old Jim sat in the tent talking about what to do and where to go to look for gold. The river was too high and too fast to pan for gold. They would have to look somewhere new.

They walked over to the bank of the river. "There goes my sluice down the river. I was going to go back and get it, but it's gone now."

"That's okay, Gold Dust, at least we got across that damn river."

"That's true; Jim, one more hour and we would have been stuck over there."

"Well, Gold Dust, where do you think we should go to find some gold?"

"What about the little creek that runs over by that big rock on the way here?"

"Young man, that's a good place to start looking."

"Jim, should we go and look today?"

"Hell no, we're going to get drunk today. It's bad luck to start looking for gold the same day you move camp."

"Okay, Jim, let's get out the bottles and get drunk."

"That's what I want to hear, young man."

"By the time we finish our bottles, we'll have so much gold that the mules will not be able to carry it all."

"That's good, Gold Dust. We can use our shovels to move all the bullshit out of the tent."

The two men had a good laugh. They began drinking and playing cards. The more they drank the taller the tales. They drank until they passed out.

In the morning, Gold Dust and Old Jim woke up with hangovers. "Gold Dust, it feels like I had one of Tim Buck's socks in my mouth all night."

"I know what you mean, Jim. I think I had one of his socks in my mouth too."

"You go and get some wood and I'll get the fire started and put some coffee on."

"Okay, Jim. I can do that and a coffee sounds good."

old Dust got some wood and came back to the tent. Old Jim had the fire started and some water on to boil.

"Hey, Gold Dust, have a drink of rum. It's a new bottle."

"No not for me, Jim. I had enough last night."

"Be a man and have a good drink. It will get the hair of the dog out of your mouth."

"You have one first, Jim. Then I'll have one."

"Goodbye hair of the dog! Boy, that was good, Gold Dust. Now you wash down the hair of the dog."

"Okay, Jim. Boy that's one rough drink before coffee."

"It opens your eyes young man and puts hair on your chest."

"That it does, Jim, and puts tears in my eyes."

The two men laughed and had some coffee and made some breakfast. Then it was time for them to work. They walked to the creek by the big rock with their mules and gold pans. Old Jim went up the creek and Gold Dust went down. By noon the rain had stopped and the sun came out. The two men went back to camp for some lunch. "Did you get any gold in that creek, young man?"

"I found a little gold, Jim. What about you? Did you find some?"

"A little, but I got this big nugget. Look at the size of it."

"That a good-sized nugget, Jim."

"That it is, young man. What's your biggest nugget for the morning?"

"Well I don't want to make you feel bad, Jim. I've got one bigger than that."

"You're full of bullshit. Let me see it."

"Here it is, Jim, it looks really good for bullshit."

"That's one big nugget. Maybe we'll have some good days in this little creek."

"Maybe we will, Jim, it would be nice."

"As long as it stays clear we'll be okay, but once it starts snowing on the mountains we may not get across the pass."

"Jim, you think the snow will melt on the pass if it stays nice?"

"I hope it does or we won't be going to Nelson. It snowed all night on the pass, and the snow is below the treelike."

"Jim, do you think Tim Buck made it over the pass today?"

"No, there's too much snow. Maybe he will wait or he may go to the next town."

"I hope he's okay, Jim. I like him."

"He'll be okay, Gold Dust. He knows the mountains."

"That's good, Jim, but what about Bucksaw?"

"Maybe the mountain ate him. It's been known to eat a man or two."

he two men had some coffee and lunch and went back to the creek to work. The sun was warm, but the air was cool. The cool air was much nicer than the wet rain. At the end of the day the two men walked back to camp. They'd worked hard all day. When they reached camp, they grabbed some wood for the night. Gold Dust was singing and Old Jim was laughing at him. Then Jim looked at him, "How much gold did you get today, young man?"

"Well I did okay, Jim."

"What's okay?"

"With what I had this morning, I have some dust and about ten nuggets."

"You must have a horseshoe up your ass, young man. I have some dust and five nuggets."

"I have the luck of forty Irishmen. I was digging under a big rock in the creek, Jim."

"You're one lucky Irishman."

"Maybe I am, Jim."

The two men ate, had a drink or two and went to sleep. Over the next five days they worked hard up and down the little creek. Gold was good for them in that little creek. They were happy with what they found. The weather was good, but it would not last much longer for the two men.

On the morning of day six at the creek the clouds rolled in. It was time for them to go back to Nelson before the snow came again on the pass. They packed up camp and started for the pass. By four in the afternoon they had reached the bottom of the pass. "Okay, Gold Dust. Let's make camp for the night."

"I'll get some wood, Jim."

Jim took the packs off the mules and dug out the coffee and some food. Then he looked up at the mountains. "Well, Gold Dust, if we don't get over tomorrow, we don't get over until spring."

"I have a beautiful woman in town waiting for me. We have to get over tomorrow."

"We will get over that damn pass tomorrow. Let's get a good night's sleep."

In the morning the two men began their long trek up the trail to the pass. By the time they reached the top it had begun snowing and the wind was blowing. There was a good foot of old snow on the trail, and about six inches of new.

"Well, Gold Dust, we can keep going or go back now. If we keep going, there's no turning back."

"Let's keep going, Jim."

"Okay. That snow is going to get bad before we get across the pass. Then we have to go down."

"That's okay, if we can get across there's a nice cave at the bottom, Jim."

"Let's go then, it's going to be a long hard trudge ahead for us."

Chapter Sixteen

The two men trudged in the snow as they began the long trek across the top of the pass. The wind and snow was getting really bad. Gold Dust let Paddy walk in front of them. That mule knew where to go.

"Jim, maybe we should have turned back."

"Well, it's too late. Now we have to keep going."

When they reached about halfway, Paddy walked to an overhang on the side of the mountain. The two men and their mules stood under the overhang to keep out some of the bad weather. Jim pulled out a bottle of rum, had a good drink and passed it to Gold Dust. As they stood having a smoke, something ran by them on the trail.

"What the hell was that, Jim?"

"I don't know, but it has a strong smell to it."

"It can run fast. Look at it go through the snow on the trail, Jim."

"Look, Gold Dust, it stopped and it's looking at us. Look how big it is."

"It can't be a man, Jim, it's too damn big."

"I've been in these mountains for more than twenty-five years, and I've never seen one, but I've talked to some prospectors that have."

"Seen what, Jim?"

"One of them Sasquatch, or what they call Bigfoot."

"Sasquatch? Bigfoot? I thought that was a tall tale, Jim."

"I thought it was too much rum in them prospectors, but I was wrong."

"It must be twelve feet tall, Jim."

"I had to see one to believe it, Gold Dust. You are one lucky man to see a Sasquatch. When you get old, you can tell your grandkids that you seen a Sasquatch in Canada."

"He's going along the trail. Maybe we can walk in the path he made in the snow."

"Okay, Gold Dust, but keep your gun close we don't want that Sasquatch to have us for its next meal."

"You think it will eat us?"

"No, but some of the prospectors had a Sasquatch throwing big rocks on their cabin one day. They had to leave their claim, and no one will go up there."

"You think it will throw rocks at us?"

"I don't know, Gold Dust, but let's keep our eyes sharp."

"Let's get going, Jim, we have to get to the bottom before dark."

"Okay, Gold Dust, let's go."

As they trudged along the trail, the two men kept a very sharp eye. Then the mules stopped, and would not move.

"What's wrong with our mules, Gold Dust?"

"They won't move, Jim, maybe something's wrong on the trail."

"Grab your gun, Gold Dust, and come with me."

"Okay, Jim, maybe the mules will come if we walk along. What the hell is that on the trail? My God, it stinks!"

"It must be Sasquatch shit, and whatever it ate was rotten before he ate it. God, that smells bad, Gold Dust."

"Let's get that shit off the trail, or the mules won't come by because it smells too bad."

"Go and get my shovel, Gold Dust."

"Okay, Jim, I can do that."

"See if you can get them mules to move."

Gold Dust went and got the shovel. "Here's your shovel, Jim. The mules came a little closer."

"God, this stinks. What does a Sasquatch eat to make it smell so bad?"

"I don't know, Jim, but it's not human to smell like this."

Old Jim moved what the Sasquatch had left for them on the trail. Gold Dust got the mules to move. They had lost some time and would have to move a little faster to get down off the pass before dark.

"Jim, that Sasquatch made a good trail in the snow for us."

"That's good, Gold Dust, maybe we'll make up for lost time."

When they reached the end of the pass and started down, the Sasquatch tracks went off into the mountain. As they trudged down the trail in two feet of snow, the two men were getting tired, cold and wet. The mules were tired too with their big packs.

"Can we stop, Jim?"

"No, Gold Dust, if we stop now we'd freeze.

Just think of that little woman in town waiting for you."

"But I'm so tired and cold, Jim."

"Me too, Gold Dust, but we have to keep moving. It will just get better as we go down the trail."

"You're right, Jim, thanks."

They keep trudging along the trail. The lower they got, the warmer it got and the less snow there was. The two men were really tired. Darkness was coming soon.

"Jim, half an hour more and we'll be at the cave."

"That's good; I can't go much longer, my old bones are hurting."

Chapter Seventeen

When they reached the cave, Jim lit a lantern. It was dry in the cave and someone had stacked a big pile of wood there. They lit a fire and took the packs off the mules. Gold Dust grabbed his bottle of whiskey, had a big drink and passed it to Old Jim.

"Gold Dust, make a bigger fire. I'm so cold after that long day in the snow."

"I can do that, Jim."

The mules stood close to the fire. They were cold and tired too. The two men were going to warm up, dry out their clothes and go to sleep.

"It was a long day, Gold Dust. How are you doing now?"

"I'm okay, Jim, but any longer and I wouldn't have made it."

"Don't feel bad, Gold Dust, an hour more and I would have had it too."

"We are two lucky men, Jim. We could have died out there today."

"That we could have, young man, but it wasn't our time to die."

They warmed up and fell asleep. Once the fire died down, it got cold in the cave. They took turns putting wood on the fire all night.

In the morning, Gold Dust was up before it was light, and had coffee on before Old Jim was awake. When it was boiled, he nudged Jim. "Get up, Jim, coffee is ready."

"Okay, I'll get up. What does it look like outside?"

"It's snowing and there's about six inches on the ground."

"I'm getting too old for this, Gold Dust. Come over here and give me a hand up."

"Are you okay, Jim?"

"My body feels like that Sasquatch kicked my ass across the pass."

"Jim, grab my hand. Maybe once you have a coffee and move around, you'll feel better."

"You're a good man, Gold Dust."

"Come over to the fire, Jim, and warm your old bones."

"Maybe that will make me feel better. Can you pass me the coffee pot, Gold Dust? I can't bend down to pick it up, it hurts too much."

"Maybe we should stay here for a day or two or until you feel better, Jim."

"No, you go to town. I'll stay here until I feel well enough to walk."

"I'm not leaving you here by yourself, Jim."

"You go, Gold Dust. If it keeps snowing, you might not get to town."

"I can leave my packs here and you can ride on Paddy. I'm not going to town without you, Jim. We made it this far together, and we'll make it all the way together. And I won't take no for an answer."

"Okay, I'll get ready."

"Okay, Jim, dress warm. It will be cold on Paddy's back."

They packed up and Gold Dust put Old Jim on the mule and began trudging in the snow for Nelson. The snow was coming down hard most of the way. In some spots the snow was three feet deep, but Gold Dust trudged along. Old Jim was not doing well, but he was hanging in there. When they got to the top of the hill outside of Nelson, there was Elephant Mountain covered with snow and the little town of Nelson.

"I can see town, Jim. We have about three hours before dark. I'll get the doctor for you when we get in."

"Good man, Gold Dust, thanks."

"Where do you live, Jim?"

"I live in my tent."

"You can't live in your tent sick as you are, Jim. You can stay with me. I have a small room in O'Donald's shop."

"You don't need an old fart like me around."

"It will be okay until you feel better."

"Thanks, Gold Dust. You make an old fool feel wanted."

"That's what friends are for, Jim."

"Not my friends, all they want is to get me to buy drinks for them."

"That's not a friend, Jim."

"I know, Gold Dust."

"It's not far now, Jim."

When they reached town, Gold Dust could see Lizzie's house and there was smoke coming out of the chimney. He couldn't wait to see her smile. When he reached O'Donald's shop, he called out, "O'Donald, give me a hand getting Old Jim off Paddy."

O'Donald ran out of his shop.

"What's wrong with Jim?"

"He's real sick. I'll go and get the doc, O'Donald."

"Go to the saloon and look there first. I seen him go over there earlier."

Gold Dust went over to the saloon to see if the doctor was there. O'Donald gave Old Jim a hand to get off Paddy. Old Jim couldn't walk by himself. He was in bad shape and O'Donald helped him to Gold Dust's room and lit a fire in the stove that he put in for Gold Dust. "Jim, are you going to make it?"

"I don't know, O'Donald, but don't tell Gold Dust how bad I am."

"Where does it hurt?"

"My whole damn body hurts like hell. Do you have any whiskey?"

"I'll get you a bottle, Jim."

"Thanks, O'Donald."

Gold Dust found the doctor in the saloon. The doctor went to O'Donald's shop. Gold Dust went to the doc's house to get his bag. When Gold Dust got back to the shop with the bag, the doctor was looking at Old Jim. "Here's your bag, Doc, how is he?"

"It could be pneumonia."

"Is he going to be okay, Doc?"

"I don't know, Gold Dust, keep him warm. I have to go to my house and get some medicine."

"Okay, Doc, I'll keep him warm."

"O'Donald, can I use your wheelbarrow?"

"What do you need a wheelbarrow for, Gold Dust?"

"I need to go and get some coal for the stove."

"You don't have to ask to use anything I have."

"I know, but I need to ask," said Gold Dust as he went and got some coal. On his way back Lizzie came running out of the hotel over to him.

"Hey, good looking, how are you doing?"

"I'm good, Lizzie, and you?"

"I'm doing much better now that you're safe in town. I didn't think you were going to make it back because of all the snow."

"I'm safe, but Old Jim is not doing too good."

"What's wrong with Jim?"

"Doc said he may have pneumonia."

"Oh dear, that's awful."

"I know, Lizzie."

"Okay, Paddy, I have to go back to work. Will you come over and see me tonight?"

"I'd love to, Lizzie. What time?"

"Would you like to come for dinner around six?"

"Okay, I'll be there for six."

Lizzie went back to work, and Gold Dust went to get the coal. On his way back to the shop he saw Bucksaw limping to the saloon. He felt badly but if Old Jim had gone down to his camp, he would have killed him. When he reached the shop, O'Donald was sitting on a bale of hay.

"Jim's sleeping now."

"Is he going to be okay, O'Donald?"

"I think if we keep him warm, he'll be okay."

"That shouldn't be hard to do. I'll keep the fire going for him."

"Come over here, sit down and tell me about your trip."

O'Donald grabbed a bottle of whiskey and the two men sat down to have a talk. The air was cool and it was raining. It would be dark in about an hour.

"I can't talk for too long, O'Donald. I have a dinner date with Lizzie."

"You're as sly as a fox, Gold Dust."

"No, I have the luck of forty Irishmen."

The two men had a little laugh and a drink.

"I stayed in the cave on my way up before going over the pass."

"It's a nice cave isn't it, Gold Dust?"

"That it is. It was nice to get out of the cold wet weather for the night."

"Let's get you cleaned up for Lizzie."

"Okay, I guess I smell like Old Jim's mule."

"Well, you don't smell like a bed of roses. I'll make a fire under the tub for you, Gold Dust."

"I'll get some coal on the fire and see how Old Jim's doing."

O'Donald got the tub ready. The water didn't take long to heat up. When Gold Dust got back from seeing to Jim, he sat in the tub. It was nice to get the chill out of his body. He began singing Irish songs. O'Donald sat having a drink and listening to Gold Dust singing. He could see Lizzie walking over to his shop with something in her hands. When she reached his shop, she had a big smile on her face.

Chapter Eighteen

"Hi, O'Donald, I have some chicken soup for you and Old Jim."

"Why thank you, Lizzie."

"Is Paddy here?"

"That's him singing in the back of the shop."

"You think it's okay to go back and see him?"

"Oh yes, it will be fine. He'll be glad to see you."

She could hear singing as she walked to the back of the shop. When she walked around the corner she stopped and laughed, "Hi, good looking."

Gold Dust turned as red as a tomato. "Hi, Lizzie, was O'Donald out there when you came in?"

"He was, but he didn't tell me you were in the tub."

"O'Donald! I'll get you back!"

"You be nice to him, Gold Dust. I'll see you later with your clothes on."

As Lizzie walked out of the shop, she was laughing, "See you, O'Donald."

"Okay, Lizzie, you have a good night."

"I will."

O'Donald had a good laugh. Then out came Gold Dust from the back of the shop. He had a big smile on his face and was shaking his head, "You didn't tell Lizzie I was in the tub."

"No, Gold Dust, she just asked who was singing and if she could go back and see you."

The two men laughed, had a drink and talked some more about Gold Dust's trip.

"Was there a lot of snow on the pass when you went over to the valley?"

"About two feet on the top; it was blowing the snow around and cold as hell. Have you seen Tim Buck in town?"

"No, I haven't. Was he with you and Old Jim?"

"He was, but he left for the pass five days ago."

"Maybe he couldn't get over the pass and went to the next valley."

"He said if he couldn't get over he was going to the next town."

"That's where he is."

"Okay, O'Donald, I have to go to Lizzie's now."

"You have fun. I'll see you later, Gold Dust."

Gold Dust walked over to Lizzie's house. The night air was cold. He was a happy man going to see a beautiful woman. When he reached her house, he could see her through the window. He stopped and watched her from the pathway. Then he walked up to the door. Before he could knock, the door opened and Lizzie's smile greeted him.

"Come in, Paddy."

"Thanks, Lizzie, you look pretty tonight."

"Why thank you, and you look handsome tonight. Come sit in the kitchen and I'll get you a drink."

"That sounds good."

"Here you go, Paddy, I've made a deer stew. I hope you like it."

"I haven't had deer from Canada before, but a deer's a deer, and I like deer meat."

"You're a bit early. It will be about one hour before dinner, but we can sit in the parlor and talk if you'd like to, Paddy."

"I'd like that, Lizzie."

The two lovebirds sat and talked in the parlor until it was time to eat. After eating, Gold Dust helped with the dishes. The two lovebirds laughed and played while they cleaned up the kitchen. Then they went back to the parlor and sat down and talked. "It must be lonely here by yourself, Lizzie?"

"It is sometimes, Paddy."

"What keeps you here?"

"I have no place to go."

"Don't you have any family around here?"

"Not around here. I have an aunt and uncle on the coast, if they're still alive."

"Am I asking too many questions, Lizzie?"

"No, Paddy, that's okay. It's nice to have someone my age to talk to."

"There're not too many people our age around here, Lizzie."

"You're right, there's not."

"Have you tried to get a hold of your aunt and uncle?"

"I have by writing, but I got no answer."

"That's all the family you have?"

"My mom's and dad's parents are dead. There's only my mom's sister and her husband, and I can't find them."

"It must be hard for you to get by with what money you make cooking at the hotel."

It is sometimes, but when there is money in town, I do okay."

"Have you every thought of moving?"

"I did after mom died, but O'Donald talked me out of it, and I'm glad he did."

"Why is that, Lizzie?"

"I had nowhere to go to. At least I have a home here and some people I know."

"I'm glad you stayed."

"Why, Paddy?"

Gold Dust began to get nervous and blurted out, "I have to go and look in on Old Jim."

"Okay, Paddy, I have to get up early in the morning."

The two lovebirds walked to the door. "Thanks for a great dinner, Lizzie."

"Will I see you tomorrow, Paddy?"

"I'd like that, Lizzie."

Lizzie gave him a big hug, a kiss on the lips and ran in the house.

Chapter Nineteen

Now Gold Dust was smiling from ear to ear as he walked back to O'Donald's shop. When he reached the shop, he could see O'Donald working.

"Why are you working at this time of the night?"

"I didn't want to go over to the saloon by myself."

"Have you looked in on Jim?"

"I was just in playing cards with him. He's sleeping now and I put some coal in the stove."

"Thanks, O'Donald."

"Come on, young man. Let's go over to the saloon to have a drink and a talk."

"Okay, that sounds good."

The two men walked over to the saloon. When they got inside, they were greeted by the girls and some prospectors. They walked over to the far corner of the saloon and sat at O'Donald's table. Lucky and Happy came over with a bottle of whiskey.

Would you two handsome men like to have some fun tonight?"

"Not tonight, girls, but you can leave that bottle of whiskey on the table."

The girls left the whiskey on the table and went back to work.

"So, Gold Dust, did you see Bucksaw in the valley? He came into town with a bullet hole in his leg."

"We did. He was digging in Old Jim's packs."

"Why was he digging in his packs?" "We think he was looking for gold. Old Jim was going to kill him."

"What stopped him?"

"I did. We were up on the bank above Jim's camp looking down at him. Jim told me to shoot him in the leg, or he was going to go down and kill him, so I did."

O'Donald began laughing. Then Gold Dust started laughing. As the two man laughed, Bucksaw limped over to their table and sat down.

"O'Donald, you think I could get a drink of that whiskey?"

"Go ahead, Bucksaw; have you met Gold Dust?"

"No I haven't. You're the one that shot that robber."

"That's me, Bucksaw."

"What were you two laughing about?"

"We were talking about someone going through Old Jim's packs."

"Well, I have to go and play some cards now."

"Stay and have one more drink, Bucksaw."

"That's okay, O'Donald, I have to go." Bucksaw hurried off.

The two men began laughing so much that they had tears running down their cheeks as Bucksaw limped away. Then Big Foot came over with a bottle and sat down.

"How is Jim doing, O'Donald?"

"He's really sick. The doc thinks it's pneumonia."

"If there's something I can do, let me know."

"You can stop in and see him, Big Foot."

"Where is he staying, Gold Dust?"

"He's in my room at the back of O'Donald's shop."

"Maybe I'll go over and see him now if he's awake."

"If you go over, can you put some coal in the stove?"

"I'll do that, Gold Dust."

"Thanks, Big Foot."

Big Foot left the saloon to go and see Old Jim.

"Guess what we seen when we were going over the pass, O'Donald?"

"I don't know, maybe you seen a bear."

"No, it wasn't a bear. We seen a Sasquatch!"

"A Sasquatch! How close was it?"

"It was close enough that we could smell it, about ten feet. It ran right past us. Then it stopped on the trail and took a big dump. The mules wouldn't go past it. We had to move it off the trail, but it stunk bad, really bad."

"You seen one of them, not too many people have seen a Sasquatch."

"It was about ten feet tall and it could run fast. Old Jim said that this was the first one he's seen."

"Jim's been walking in the mountains for years."

"Has anyone been eaten by a Sasquatch?"

"Not that I know of, but some prospectors had rocks thrown at their cabins."

"Did anyone get hurt?"

"No, but they won't go back to their cabins."

"I don't think I would go back if it was my cabin."

"Gold Dust, how long did it take you and Jim to get back over the pass?"

"All day; there was two feet of snow on the pass and it was snowing and blowing and cold as hell."

"It must have been hard to see."

"It was. We had to let Paddy walk in the front. By the time we got to the cave we could not walk any more. One more hour and we would be frozen on the trail somewhere."

"I guess it was too much for Old Jim, all that cold and wet."

"It was, O'Donald, way too much."

"You know he's sixty years old. That's why they call him Old Jim."

"I had to help him up in the morning. He told me to leave him there and that he would come to town when he was better."

"He'd be dead by now, Gold Dust."

"I guess he would be, O'Donald."

The two men sat in the saloon drinking and talking for hours. Finally Gold Dust just couldn't keep his eyes open any longer and yawned, "I have to get some sleep; it's been a long day."

"I guess it has been for you, Gold Dust."

"It has, O'Donald."

O'Donald and Gold Dust walked back to the shop. "I'll see you in the morning, O'Donald."

"Have a good sleep, Gold Dust."

Gold Dust went to his little room and put some coal in the stove. Old Jim was sleeping and he was snoring loudly. Gold Dust was so tired that he fell asleep even with Old Jim snoring.

Chapter Twenty

In the morning Gold Dust got up, put some coffee on and looked at Jim. "It's time for you to wake up, Jim."

"What time is it, young man?"

"It's time for you to take your medicine."

"I guess I should."

"Come on, open up. It's good for you, Jim."

"Boy, it tastes bad!"

"Don't be a baby, Jim, it's not that bad."

"You try it if it's not that bad."

"That's okay, Jim, are you hungry?"

"I could eat something, Gold Dust."

"Lizzie brought some chicken soup over last night."

"That girl makes a good chicken soup."

"I'll warm some up for you."

"Thanks, Gold Dust. If you would have left me in that cave, I'd be dead now."

"You're welcome, Jim." Gold Dust warmed up some soup and gave some to Jim. "I'm going to have breakfast at the hotel. I'll see you later."

"Okay, I'll see you."

Gold Dust walked over to the hotel and had some breakfast. He talked with Lizzie. Then he went back to O'Donald's shop.

"Morning, Gold Dust. How is Jim doing?"

"He seems to be doing better. He ate some of that chicken soup."

"That sounds good. How did you sleep?"

"It was okay, but Jim can snore loud. It was a good thing I was really tired."

"What are you going to do today, young man?"

"I have to sell my gold and mail a letter to my mom."

"Do you think you can give me a hand in the shop later?"

"I can do that for you, O'Donald, when I get back."

"Thanks, Gold Dust."

Gold Dust went and sold his gold and gave the man shit for telling everyone that someone had found gold in the next valley. Then he walked back to the shop.

"What do you need a hand with, O'Donald?"

"I have to take a load of metal plates up to the silver mine."

"I can help you do that."

"Can we use Paddy to pull the wagon?"

"I'll hook Paddy to the wagon and bring him over here."

"Thanks, Gold Dust. That will make my job a little easier."

The two men loaded the wagon with the metal plates and went up to the mine. It was a long walk. When they reached the mine, Gold Dust had a look around. It looked like hard and dangerous work. Then he went and helped O'Donald unload the wagon.

"Okay, Gold Dust, let's go back to town. We can ride in the wagon and have a drink or two of whiskey on the way down."

"It will be better than walking, and a drink sounds good."

The two men sat in the wagon as Paddy walked back to town. They talked and drank all the way down. It was a warm winter day and it looked like it was going to be nice for awhile. Over the next ten days it was warm and all the snow in town had melted. Gold Dust had seen a lot of Lizzie. He was a very happy man. Old Jim was feeling better and getting around. It was time for Gold Dust to go and get his packs out of the cave.

Chapter Twenty-One

"I'm going to the cave to get my packs, O'Donald."

"You be careful going up there. All this warm weather is good for snow slides."

"I'll be careful. I'll have Paddy with me. He'll let me know if it's not safe."

"I'm going to come with you, Gold Dust."

"No, you're not, Jim."

"I'm feeling well enough to go with you."

"Jim, you're going to stay here if I have to tie you to the bed."

"Okay, I'll stay but you damn well be careful. I don't want to go up there and dig you out of a snow bank."

"Okay, you two sound like my dad. I'm going to go and say goodbye to Lizzie. I'll see you in two days."

O'Donald called out to Gold Dust, "If you're not back in two days, we'll be coming to look for you."

Gold Dust walked down to Lizzie's house to say goodbye. "Morning, Lizzie, I'm going to go and get my packs from the cave."

"You be careful, Paddy, I don't want to lose you in the mountains."

"I'll be okay."

Lizzie gave him a kiss and a hug, and said goodbye. Gold Dust walked up the hill out of town. When he reached the top of the hill, he stopped and looked back at the little town and Elephant Mountain.

He scratched between his mule's ears, "Paddy, we have to go and look on that mountain for gold when we get back. Come on, Paddy, we have a good walk ahead of us."

It was a beautiful winter day as they walked along the trail. By noon he was walking in snow. All the little creeks were small rivers from all the snow melting. They walked over some snow slides that covered the trail. Gold Dust was a little nervous and he could feel that Paddy was too. As they walked along, they could hear snow slides in the mountains.

When they reached the cave, Gold Dust made a fire to dry his clothes that got wet crossing the small rivers. He put on some coffee and made something to eat. He talked as he ate, "Well Paddy, I hope we get back tomorrow."

Gold Dust could hear the rumbling in the mountains. He was hoping that there would not be a slide on the trail and that he'd be able to get back to Nelson.

Then there was a loud rumble and the cave began shaking. "What the hell is that, Paddy?"

Then everything was quiet. Gold Dust grabbed his gun and walked out of the cave. "Come on, Paddy, let's go have a look. I hope that slide is up the trail and not down the trail."

They walked down the trail for ten minutes but didn't see a slide. Then they walked back to the cave and up the trail five minutes. There it was - a huge slide over the trail with trees and rocks mixed in the snow!

"We are lucky, Paddy, that we are going down the trail; not up."

They walked back to the cave, but Gold Dust was a little nervous. They would have to get up early and hope the trail was open. He put some more wood on the fire and grabbed his bottle of whiskey. "Too bad you don't drink, Paddy, you could probably use one right now. Here's to you, Paddy, you're a good mule."

Paddy walked over to him and put his nose on the bottle. "Do you want a drink, Paddy?" Gold Dust opened up the bottle. "Have a drink, but don't get sick."

To Gold Dust's surprise that mule grabbed the bottle and would not let go! "Give me that bottle, Paddy! You don't have to drink it all. I need some too!" Gold Dust laughed as he got the bottle from Paddy. He had drunk over half the bottle of whiskey. "Did Old Jim teach you how to drink? I hope there isn't any backwash in this bottle." Gold Dust had a good laugh and got his bed made. "Okay you crazy mule, I'll see you in the morning with no hangover! We have to get to town!" He laughed at Paddy and lay down for the night.

In the morning they were up before light. Gold Dust made coffee and had breakfast. It was cold up on the mountainside. At the crack of dawn they were on the trail. If they could get down the trail far enough, there would be less chance of a slide. As they walked along the trail, Gold Dust could see some new slides that had happened after he came past the day before. They were small slides and not hard to get over. As the sun came up on the mountains, he could hear the rumble in the distance.

"We have to move fast, Paddy."

Paddy stopped. "What is it, Paddy?"

Then Gold Dust could hear a rumble. It was too close. The ground began to shake.

"Paddy, let's go over to that huge rock. Hurry!" As they stood behind the huge rock, Gold Dust could see up the side of the mountain. He watched the rocks and snow come down, taking down everything in its path. He had never seen anything with so much force. It shook the ground as it came down. It was hard for Gold Dust and Paddy to stand up. Some of the rocks were hitting the huge rock they were behind!

"It's going to be okay, Paddy. We'll stay right here and we'll be okay." Gold Dust was really nervous. Maybe he should have stayed in town.

When the slide was over, the trail was one big mess. Gold Dust could maybe get over the slide, but there was no way that Paddy would get over. "Okay, Paddy, I'm not going to leave you here by yourself. We can find somewhere to get over. Come on let's go and look up first."

They worked their way up. It was hard climbing. After an hour of climbing they stopped. Gold Dust sat on a rock and lit a smoke. "Well, Paddy, what a mess I've got us in."

He sat smoking and thinking of Lizzie, and that if he didn't get back O'Donald and Old Jim would come looking for him. Then he looked around for Paddy and couldn't see him. "Where are you? Come over here."

Then Paddy came out from behind a big rock. "Did you find a way over the slide? If you did, I'll buy you a bottle of whiskey and a big bag of oats." Gold Dust got up and walked over to Paddy. "Okay, you show me the way over this damn slide."

They worked their way over the slide and back down to the trail. It took them four hours. This meant that they were about four hours behind. As they walked along they could hear the rumble behind them. Then they came to a small slide. It took some time to get over it, but they did. It looked like it would be okay now. The slides looked like they were behind them.

As they walked, Gold Dust could see someone down the trail a ways. "Who do you think that is way down there, Paddy?" Gold Dust could see them every now and then as he came down the trail. Then around a corner came two people with a mule. When they got close enough to see who it was, he could not believe his eyes! It was O'Donald and Lizzie!

"What are you two doing here?"

"We came to see if you were okay."

"I'm okay, Lizzie." Lizzie gave him a big hug and a kiss. "I'm glad you're okay, Paddy. We could hear the rumbling in town."

"Okay, you two lovebirds, let's get going. I'll get my kiss later, Paddy."

"Okay, O'Donald, but it's Gold Dust and no kiss for you."

As they walked back to town, Gold Dust was happy he had someone to talk with. When they reached the hill outside of town, it was getting dark.

"One more hour and we would have been caught in the dark, Gold Dust."

"We are lucky, O'Donald."

They walked down the hill and into town. Old Jim was standing by O'Donald's shop and shouted to them, "You made it, Gold Dust. I thought you might have been caught up in them damn mountains!"

"It was close, but we got out, Jim."

"Paddy, I'm going home."

"I'll walk with you, Lizzie."

"That would be nice."

Lizzie and Gold Dust walked to her house. They stood outside and talked for awhile.

"I have to go and get some sleep, Lizzie. It's been a long day for me."

"Okay, Paddy, I'll see you tomorrow."

"I'll come over to the hotel for breakfast in the morning."

Lizzie gave him a hug and a kiss, and went in her house. Gold Dust walked back to O'Donald's shop.

"Well, young man, are you coming to the saloon?"

"No, not tonight, I have to get some sleep."

"Okay, Gold Dust, I'll see you in the morning."

"Where's Old Jim?"

"He's got a room at the saloon."

"Okay I'll sleep in my bed tonight."

Gold Dust went to his room and got the bed ready. "It will be nice to sleep in a bed." As he lay in bed, he thanked God for getting him back safe and went to sleep.

Chapter Twenty-Two

In the morning he was up early, put some coffee on, and walked to the front of the shop. He looked up at Elephant Mountain and smiled. There was a little snow on the top, but he had to go up on that mountain before the next snowfall. The weather had warmed up and most of the snow was gone. Maybe he could get a week or two on the mountain before it snowed again. He went back and grabbed a cup of coffee and walked back to the front of the shop.

"What are you looking at, young man?"

"Morning, O'Donald, I'm looking at that mountain."

"You're not thinking of going up there, are you?"

"I think I'm going to go and have a look."

"That's not a good idea, Gold Dust."

"Why?"

"The weather could turn bad overnight, and you could get caught up there."

"I think I'm going to go up tomorrow."

"You're too hungry for gold, young man."

"No, I'm not. I need to go up and see, O'Donald. I dream about that damn mountain every night."

"Okay, if you need to go, only go for one week."

"I'll only go for a week. Come on, I have some coffee on."

"That sounds good, Gold Dust."

The two men sat and talked over a coffee.

"Are you coming for breakfast? I'm buying."

Am I coming for breakfast? Does an Irishman ever pass up a meal?"

They had a little laugh and walked over to the hotel. When they walked in, Lizzie was hard at work. "Good morning, boys."

"Morning, Lizzie."

"What are you two handsome men going to have?"

"I'll have what I always have."

"Okay, O'Donald. What about you, Paddy?"

"I'll have the same as O'Donald."

"Coffee for you two?"

"Please. That will be nice, Lizzie."

The two men had breakfast and talked about how cold the winters can get in Nelson. Then they walked back to O'Donald's shop. "Do you need a hand with anything today, O'Donald?"

"Maybe you can get me some coal from Blacky's."

"Okay, I can do that for you."

"Hook-up Paddy to the wagon."

"How much coal do you need?"

"Ten bags will do. Tell Blacky I'll be over to pay him later."

"Okay, O'Donald."

Gold Dust hooked Paddy to the wagon and went to get some coal from Blacky. On his way over he could see a crowd gathering on the street. When he reached the crowd, he worked his way through to see Old Jim and Bucksaw yelling at each other. "What are you two arguing about?"

"Gold Dust, you tell this damn fool that I didn't shoot him in the leg."

"He didn't shoot you in the leg, Bucksaw. If he was going to shoot at you, you'd be dead now."

"What's going on here?"

"Jim shot me in the leg, Sheriff."

"Slow down, Bucksaw. Well, Jim, did you shoot him?"

"No, Sheriff, if I was going to shoot him, he'd be dead."

"I shot him, Sheriff."

Bucksaw and the Sheriff looked at Gold Dust. The crowd came silent and they all looked at Gold Dust.

"See, I told you I didn't shoot you."

"Why did you shoot him?"

"We saw him digging through Jim's packs from on top of the river bank. Jim was going to go down and kill him if I didn't shoot him in the leg."

"Were you digging in Jim's packs, Bucksaw?" Bucksaw hemmed and hawed as everyone looked at him. "Well, Bucksaw, were you in Jim's camp digging in his packs?"

"I was, Sheriff, but I was looking for some coffee."

"The hell you were!" Jim shouted.

"Okay, Jim."

"He was looking for my gold, Sheriff."

"You're lucky, Bucksaw, that Jim didn't come down from the river bank. He would have killed you."

"I guess I am, Sheriff."

"Okay, it's all over. You folks can all go about your business."

Everyone went on their way. Old Jim stood looking at the ground.

"Well, Jim, you got everyone in town on the streets."

"I guess I did, Gold Dust."

"Maybe you should go and sleep this one off."

"I guess I should. I'll see you later."

"Okay, Jim."

Gold Dust walked away shaking his head. When he reached Blacky's he could see some bags of coal in his shop.

"Can I help you?"

"I'm over to pick up some coal for O'Donald."

"How many bags does he need?"

"Ten will do, and he will be over later to pay you, Blacky."

"Tell O'Donald I'll have a bottle of whiskey here for him."

"I can do that for you, Blacky."

Chapter Twenty-Three

On his way back to O'Donald's shop, he could see Bucksaw walking towards him. "Gold Dust, can I talk to you?"

"What can I do for you, Bucksaw?"

"Well, thanks for not letting Jim shoot me back in the valley."

"I feel bad about shooting you in the leg."

"That's okay, Gold Dust, at least I'm alive." The two men talked for a bit then went on their way. As Gold Dust walked along with Paddy, he could see O'Donald standing in front of his shop. "What was the crowd about earlier, Gold Dust?"

"It was Old Jim and Bucksaw arguing."

"What the hell were those two fools arguing about?"

"I think the whiskey had something to do with the argument. Bucksaw thought Jim shot him in the leg."

"He's lucky you shot him. Jim would have killed him and put his body in a hole."

"They were arguing at the saloon late last night. I talked to the Sheriff. He told Bucksaw he was lucky to be alive."

"That he is, Gold Dust. If you weren't there with Jim, he would have killed him."

"What a couple of old fools they are, O'Donald." They had a good laugh. "Where would you like this coal put?"

"Just put it in that corner."

"Come on, Paddy, let's get this unloaded and take this wagon off." Gold Dust unloaded the wagon, put it back behind the shop and unhooked Paddy. He put Paddy in a corral and gave him some oats. "Go and play with Old Jim's mule, Paddy. I'll see you later today."

"O'Donald, I'm going to get some supplies for tomorrow."

"Okay, I'll see you when you get back. Oh, could you pickup some jerky for me?"

"Okay, I can do that for you."

As Gold Dust walked to get his supplies, he looked up at that mountain. "I'll be up on the top tomorrow."

As he walked past the saloon, Big Foot walked out. He was a big man with feet as big as snowshoes. He had to get shoes specially made to fit his feet.

"Gold Dust, I heard that you shot Bucksaw!"

"I did, Big Foot."

"That's good you shot that old fool. I caught him in my camp two months ago. He said he was looking for coffee, but I think he was looking for my gold."

"That's what he told the Sheriff, that he was looking for coffee."

"Come in and have a drink with the boys."

"Maybe later, I have some things to do, Big Foot."

"Okay, Gold Dust, maybe later."

Gold Dust got his supplies and walked back to O'Donald's shop. "Here's your jerky. Oh, Blacky said he had a bottle of whiskey waiting for you."

"Great, I'll go over and help him with that bottle."

"Could you have a look at Paddy's shoes?"

"I'll do that before going over to Blacky's."

"Thanks, I'm going to put my supplies in my packs."

Gold Dust put his supplies in his packs and got everything ready for morning. "Well I'm ready to go up that mountain tomorrow, O'Donald."

"I still think you should wait until spring to go up that damn mountain, young man."

"I'll be okay. If it starts to snow, I'll come back down."

"Are you going up the backside? It's not as steep as this side."

"Maybe I will. I should be able to cross the river on the rail trestles."

"You can, Gold Dust. It's a little longer walk but it will be safer than going up the steep side."

"There's still snow on this side; it doesn't get much sun."

"It makes me feel a little better that you're going up the backside."

"I'll be okay, O'Donald. I'm going over to Lizzie's for the rest of the day."

"Okay, you have fun."

As Gold Dust walked to Lizzie's house, he looked up at Elephant Mountain. I'll be on top of you tomorrow."

Chapter Twenty - Four

It was warm in the little town that day. Gold Dust spent the rest of the day with Lizzie, walking down by the river.

"Lizzie, I'm going up Elephant Mountain in the morning."

"Is that a good idea to go up there at this time of the year? What if it starts snowing when you're up there?"

"I'll be okay. If it starts to snow, I'll come back to town."

"I don't like it, but you're old enough to do what you want to."

"I have to go and see if there is gold on that mountain. I dream about that mountain every night."

"Well, Paddy, a man's got to do what a man's got to do."

The two lovebirds had a good laugh and started back to Lizzie's house. Hand in hand they walked. "Would you like to come in, Paddy?"

"Okay, that would be nice, Lizzie."

"I have to get ready to work, Paddy."

"You're working tonight?"

"I have to help May bake some pies for tomorrow. It would be nice if you walked me."

"I'd like that, Lizzie, maybe I'll have something to eat when we get there."

I think May made some stew for tonight."

"That sounds good to me."

"Paddy, can you help me do up this zipper on my dress?"

His face turned red and he could not talk.

"Paddy, you can come in the bedroom. Are you still here?"

"I am, Lizzie."

"Can you do that for me?"

"Okay, I'll be right there." When he opened the door and walked into the bedroom, Lizzie turned and smiled at him. Her long, golden blond hair was shining in the light of the lamp. Gold Dust stopped. You look beautiful, Lizzie."

"Thanks, Paddy. That means a lot to me."

"Here, let me see if I can get that zipper to work. There, I think it's working now."

Lizzie turned around and gave him a big kiss and a hug. "Thanks, Paddy."

138

"Thank you, Lizzie. I needed that kiss and hug."

"Me too, Paddy, maybe we can do some more kissing and hugging later."

"That sounds like fun, Lizzie."

"It does, Paddy. I have to get to work now."

The two lovebirds walked over to the hotel.

"I'm going to see if O'Donald would like to come and eat with me."

"Okay, don't be long. I'll have some stew ready."

Gold Dust walked over to O'Donald's shop.

When he reached the shop, O'Donald was sitting on a bale of hay reading a letter.

"Who's the letter from?"

"It's from my folks."

"How are they doing?"

"They're doing great. I thought you were going to spend the rest of the day with Lizzie?"

"I am. I just came to see if you would like to come and have some dinner with me. I'm buying."

"Okay, that sounds like a good idea, Gold Dust."

The two men walked over to the hotel, went in and sat down. Lizzie came from the kitchen with a big smile on her face. "Okay, you two, I'll get two bowls of stew."

"Thanks, Lizzie."

The two men ate and talked; Lizzie was hard at work in the kitchen.

"Well, Gold Dust, are you coming over to the saloon to bullshit a bit?"

"I think I will. Lizzie, how long are you going to be?"

"Are you going to the saloon with O'Donald?"

"I'm thinking of it, if you're going to be awhile."

"I'm going to be about four hours."

"Okay, I'll come back and walk you home."

"No kissing other girls, you have to save your kisses for me."

O'Donald began laughing. Gold Dust's face turned red. Then they all had a little laugh.

"I'll make sure he behaves himself, Lizzie. I'll get all the kisses from the girls."

"I know you will, O'Donald. You boys go and play now and behave yourselves."

As they were leaving, Lizzie gave Gold Dust a big kiss and a hug. "Will that keep you going until you get back, Paddy?"

"That will, Lizzie."

"Where is my kiss, Lizzie?"

"Come here, O'Donald." Lizzie gave O'Donald a hug and a kiss on the cheek.

Then the two men walked over to the saloon.

When they walked in, the smoke was heavy and the bullshit was thick from the crowd of prospectors drinking and swapping tales. They walked to the far corner of the saloon to O'Donald's table. Old Jim and Big Foot were sitting at the table.

"Well, you two old fools, how are you tonight?"

"Okay, O'Donald, if we were in the mountains with all this bullshit, we'd have so much gold that the mules wouldn't be able the carry it." They all had a good laugh. "Sit down you two. Happy and Lucky are coming over. Maybe you'll get lucky with Lucky, Gold Dust."

"Gold Dust has to be good tonight, no kissing the girls."

"Who told you that, O'Donald?"

"Lizzie did. I have to make sure he behaves himself."

"Well, Gold Dust, it looks like we have to do your job."

"That's okay. At least I'll have some money in my pocket in the morning."

The four men had a good laugh.

"Hi, Gold Dust, do you feel like Happy tonight?"

"Not tonight, Happy."

"What about Lucky and Happy."

"No girls, you will have to be happy with Old Jim and Big Foot for tonight."

"You're more fun than them, Gold Dust."

They all had a laugh.

"Well, O'Donald, could you use a good woman or maybe two for the night?"

"Not tonight, Gold Dust. We have to give these two old fools a chance with the girls."

"We're not too old, O'Donald. There may be snow on the roof, but there's still some fire in the furnace."

They had a good laugh at Old Jim and Big Foot. Gold Dust sat and laughed as he listened to the stories and drank with the old boys. Then it was time to go and walk Lizzie home and get some kissing and hugging.

Chapter Twenty - Five

As he walked over to the hotel, he was thinking how lucky he was to have made some good friends in Nelson, so far from home. When he walked up to the door, he could see Lizzie cleaning the tables. He stopped and looked at her for a bit.

When he walked in and smiled at her, she smiled back at him. "I'll be ready in a minute, Paddy."

"No rush, Lizzie, I can wait."

"Okay, I'm done, let's go."

The two lovebirds walked over to Lizzie's house. When they got inside, Lizzie lit a lamp and Gold Dust made a fire. It was cold in the house, but it didn't take too long to warm up. Lizzie grabbed a bottle of whiskey and two glasses and sat them on the table. "Okay, Paddy, come and sit with me."

"I'll be right there, Lizzie."

"It's been a long day, Paddy. Can you rub my neck a little?"

"I can do that for you."

As he put his hand on her neck he was a little nervous. Her skin was soft and smooth. As he rubbed shoulders, she talked to him. The two lovebirds were very happy. "Paddy, it's time we do some hugging and kissing. I'll turn off some of the lamps. That minister comes and looks in my windows to see if there's a man in here with me."

"He shouldn't be looking in your windows."

"I know, so let's go into my bedroom and close the door. He can't see in that room."

"That minister is one sick minister."

"Come on. I need to work on my kissing, Paddy."

"Okay, that sounds like fun to me."

"I have to get out of this dress and put on a clean one. Can you help with this zipper again?"

"What would the minister think if he saw us in your bedroom and me unzipping your dress?"

"He'd have something to talk about on Sunday in church."

"Okay, you turn around and I'll put on a clean dress."

"Okay, Lizzie."

"Okay, you can turn around now."

"That's a pretty dress!"

"Thanks, Paddy, now let's go to work and do some kissing and hugging!"

"Okay, I like that kind of work." The two lovebirds kissed and hugged for hours.

I'm going to need some sleep so I can work tomorrow, Paddy."

"I guess my lips need to get some sleep too, Lizzie."

The two lovebirds laughed.

"We have to do this when you get back, Paddy."

"I'd love that, Lizzie."

"Okay, come by the hotel before you go up that mountain."

"I will."

"Thanks, I had a great night, but I have to work on my kissing a little more."

"No. You do a great job."

"Okay, you go now, Paddy, or I may do something I shouldn't."

"Okay."

Gold Dust sneaked out of the house and walked to his room. It was late and he had a long day ahead. When he reached his room, he was thinking that maybe he should stay in town so he could be with Lizzie. He knew if he stayed he would dream of

Elephant Mountain all winter. He would have to go up that mountain.

In the morning he was a little tired, but he knew he had to get ready. He walked over to the hotel. When he walked in, he could see O'Donald sitting at a table. "Morning, Gold Dust, how are you this morning?"

"I'm good, O'Donald, a little tired though."

"Lizzie is a little tired too." O'Donald had a little laugh.

"Come on and sit down and get some coffee in you."

"Morning, good looking, need some coffee?"

"That I do, Lizzie. I have to wake up."

"Maybe you should have gone home earlier last night."

"No, Lizzie, I had a great night with you."

"I had a great night too, but I'm a little tired too."

"What did you two do last night?"

"We sat and talked all night."

"I bet you just talked."

They all had a laugh.

"I'll get you something to eat, Paddy. What would you like for breakfast?"

"You surprise me, Lizzie."

Lizzie went in the kitchen to make Gold Dust's breakfast.

"Well, young man, I still think you should wait until spring to go up that mountain."

"That's what Lizzie said to me."

"You have one week up on that mountain."

The two men talked as Lizzie made breakfast for Gold Dust.

"Here you go, Paddy. You eat all of this."

"Okay, Lizzie, I'm as hungry as a bear."

"Did you mean hungry as a horse?"

"No. I feel like a bear."

O'Donald and Lizzie laughed at Gold Dust.

"You eat up, Paddy. I have to go back in the kitchen."

Gold Dust ate and talked to O'Donald. Then it was time to go. He caught Lizzie's eye. "Lizzie, I'm going now."

"You be careful on that mountain."

"I will, Lizzie."

She gave him a kiss and a hug. Some of the people at the tables looked in surprise.

Gold Dust and O'Donald walked out of the hotel and down the street to the shop. They put the packs on Paddy, and it was time for Gold Dust to go up Elephant Mountain. Gold Dust looked up at the mountain with determination. "I'll be on top of you today."

"Okay, you be careful going up that damn mountain. If you're not back here in one week,

I'm coming to look for you."

"I'll be okay, O'Donald. I'll see you in one week."

As Gold Dust walked out of town, O'Donald shook his head. Gold Dust had two hours to get to the backside of Elephant Mountain.

The Saga continues... in 'Elephant Mountain ~ To the Top!' ... coming soon...

~ About the Author ~

Arthur 'Art' Bruno Boudreau was born, in 1957, the fourth child in a family of six in Little River Harbour, Nova Scotia and grew up in a home his parents built on the foundation of his father's grandparents home – his father lives there still. Though his father's first language was French, English was spoken in the home in respect for his Scots born and raised mother; needless to say, attendance at the French speaking public school was a challenge.

Within this hardworking family, everyone pitched in from an early age. Art was setting snares and traps in the early mornings and carrying on through the woods to catch the school bus – shotgun and all from the time he began school. Every season brought its own industry from berry picking, fishing, duck hunting to Irish mossing. As soon as he was old enough to leave school, Art joined the family lobster fishing and worked in fishing, trapping and construction.

Live hard – play hard; that was the way of Art's growing up years. Art's first adventure away from his home territory was when he 'ran away' (or rather joined) the circus. He traveled throughout the Maritimes and saw a lot of living and learned much about human nature. Art became a life long student in the study of human nature. With that ever growing knowledge and his natural skills and abilities, he was able to get through the following decades, with his limited reading and writing skills, by working in labour industries.

~ About the Author ~

Art moved to BC about 25 years ago. He started out fishing then worked in a warehouse until a broken leg lost him his job. He lived on the streets awhile and moved to a beach. Then he went tree planting on the West Coast and the interior of B.C. and moved to Nelson. He built a cabin in the woods and lived there for three years. When he moved back to the coast on Vancouver Island he lived in a cabin on the beach where he eventually met his wife - and moved into town. *(He is still happily married with three lovely daughters.)* He got a job in a tree nursery that grew nine million seedlings a year until a work accident injuring his leg ended his physical working days. WCB would not pay him unless he was willing to go to school to learn to read and write, and so... he did!

NO DOUBT THE UNIVERSE IS UNFOLDING AS IT SHOULD

www.ingramcontent.com/pod-product-compliance
Lightning Source LLC
Chambersburg PA
CBHW030303130626
46549CB00002B/679